12-25-2

Calvin -
your Friend,

NEVER OVER THE HILL

(A Memoir in Bright Orange)

by Dan Conaway & Bill Haltom

Dan Conaway, BS, Communications, 1971
Bill Haltom, BA, History, 1975, JD, 1978

Rooster Scratch Press

Copyright 2023 © Dan Conaway and Bill Haltom, Rooster Scratch Press

Art direction: Carroll Moore
Editors: Dan Conaway and Bill Haltom
Cover photo: Steven Bridges / The University of Tennessee
Interior campus photos: Emily Styles, *BS, Advertising, Minor in Business, 2004*
   (a Memphis girl, perfect)

"For these guys, and for me, orange is a lifetime color. No matter where you went to college, this book will remind you of how that colored your life. A great read."
— **Peyton Manning**

"Anybody who attended UT during the same era as Bill Haltom and Dan Conaway can identify — while simultaneously sighing in nostalgia and gulping in embarrassment — with these riotous stories. How th'hell did we, let alone the university, survive?"

— **Sam Venable**, *Knoxville News Sentinel columnist and UT School of Journalism's least-promising graduate in the class of '69*

"What a fun book! I have no idea how Bill and Dan squeezed all the joys of college into a single book. But then, I have no idea how they squeezed the Vietnam War, the moon landing, integration, and nekkid streakers into a single book. Oh, plus stolen toilet seats and 'Rocky Top' and romance and wistfulness. So, the book is a lot like college, come to think of it. And it will stay with you, in just the same way."

— **Geoff Calkins**, *Daily Memphian columnist and morning radio host, named best sports columnist in America five times by AP Sports Editors*

"Never Over the Hill is a must read for anyone who attended college during the 1960s and 1970s regardless of where you went to school. Dan Conaway and Bill Haltom's gift for storytelling is on full display in this beautifully written book looking back at their years at UT and their look forward at the true meaning and impact of the lifelong friendships they made there."

— **Mike Wirth**, *Dean & Professor Emeritus, College of Communication and Information, University of Tennessee, Knoxville*

"Two great Volunteers reminisce about their college days at the University of Tennessee, but it is much more than that, it is great storytelling. Hilarious stories about two young men coming of age in the 60s and 70s on a college campus. It transcends time and will make each of us fondly remember our own college days, no matter the decade."

— **Margie Nichols Gill,** *Vice Chancellor for Communications Emerita, University of Tennessee, Knoxville*

To my Volunteers,
Hallie and Gaines

– Dan Conaway

In loving memory of
Jack and Nancy Reese

– Bill Haltom

AUTHORS

Dan Conaway, BS, Communications, University of Tennessee, 1971. Creative Director of UT's winning team in the 1971 American Advertising Federation Student Advertising Competition, member of the original College of Communications Board of Visitors, and recipient of the Edith S. Joel Award as Outstanding Advertising Alumnus. An award-winning communications consultant, Dan is also a columnist with The Daily Memphian, and the author of seven books, including two collections of his columns "I'm a Memphian." (Nautilus Publishing, 2013), and "In A Colorful Place" with Otis Sanford (Rooster Scratch Press, 2020).

Bill Haltom, BS, University of Tennessee, 1975, and JD, University of Tennessee, 1978. UT Torchbearer and SGA President. A lawyer who has served as President of the Tennessee Bar Association, Bill is now an award-winning columnist for the Tennessee USA Today Network, and the author of nine books, including "The Other Fellow May Be Right: The Civility of Howard Baker" (TBA Press, 2017), and "Full Court Press: How Pat Summitt and a Legal Team Changed the Game" (UT Press, 2018).

Bill Haltom and Dan Conaway

AUTHORS' NOTE

To paraphrase the TV series, *Dragnet*, a TV staple when we were kids, some of the names in our book have been changed – not to protect the innocent – but to protect the stupid from uncomfortable conversations around our Thanksgiving tables.

There are enough of those already.

Children, and grandchildren, don't necessarily have to know everything.

Besides, everybody in the book, those still with us and those who have made it to the end zone, all became respectable.

Well, mostly.

Our apologies for any misspelled names – the real ones – or juggled dates – the calendar kind – or differences in our version of events and what some of you may remember – noting that most of us can't accurately remember breakfast today.

But we can remember exactly what we had for breakfast at the Krystal on The Strip at two in the morning five decades ago, in answer to the quintessential East Tennessee question, "What fer ya?"

Two eggs over medium, bacon, waffle, order of fries, milk.

About a buck.

If you have serious problems with the content, talk to our lawyer. That would be Bill. Dan will give you his number.

Enjoy.

– Dan Conaway and Bill Haltom

FOREWORD

"On a hallowed hill in Tennessee..."

When I arrived at the University of Tennessee from Memphis in the fall of 1967, it's only appropriate that I was driven there by my father.

From the Mississippi River across the Tennessee River on I-40, across the three Grand Divisions of Tennessee, divisions of geography, divisions of commerce, divisions of thought and culture, divisions of green, from the fields of the Mississippi Delta, through the hills of Middle Tennessee through the rock walled passages leading to the foothills of the Smokies. Handwoven chenille bedspreads waved at passing cars, and shellacked surfaces of hand-carved rustic wooden furniture shown in the sun, all offered for sale.

Beyond Nashville was a brand-new world for me, the width and wonder of my state a discovery, precursor to the next four years, to the rest of my life.

It took us a hard nine hours to drive it from Memphis. There was no interstate through Nashville. We drove through town, by the Parthenon replica, by Vanderbilt, by cars with license plates that started with 2. Ours started with 1.

We were coming from the largest city in Tennessee, so that was that. And that would change.

We would pick up I-40 on the other side of Nashville but lose it again at Monterey. We drove through Cookeville on Highway 70, up on the Cumberland Plateau through Crossville, and behind every truck through the mountains in the dark, down to Rockwood, to the tall twin smokestacks of Harriman, and then picking up I-40 into Knoxville.

It had been an impossibly green day, and impossibly beautiful and frightening.

"Like a beacon shining bright..."

I was 17, 5-11, and 155 pounds of scared to death. Dad and I stayed that first night in Knoxville in a motel by the interstate, huddled around a radio, listening to the opening game of the '67 season, between Tennessee and UCLA in Los Angeles. We lost 20-16.

George Mooney called the game, so that was that. And that would change.

The next morning, we hauled my footlocker up to the second floor of the brand-new men's dorm Reese Hall. Back at the car, he gave me hug, took my shoulders, and said, "This sets the course. Make us proud."

And he was gone.

"The stately walls of old UT..."

College in 1967 at UT was little different than college for Dad in 1927 at Washington and Lee.

The same V-neck sweaters and khakis were the basic uniform, allowances made from pleats to flat fronts and back again. He wore a tie and wool blazer to his first football game, as did I. He presented his date with a corsage, as did I. She was in heels and a wool suit, as was mine. He had a flask in the pocket of that blazer, as did I. He sweat through everything, as did his date, as did I and mine.

But you switched to wool in September, so that was that. And that would change.

"Rise glorious to the sight."

The Summer of Love was 1967, but it hadn't made it to UT quite yet. It's a long way from San Francisco to Knoxville, then and now, and that distance is measured in far more than miles.

Joining a fraternity was a given for me, which one being the only question. In fact, the one I joined was founded at the Virginia Military

Academy, sharing a border with Dad's W&L, a border wall of stacked stone in Lexington, Virginia.

My fraternity, Alpha Tau Omega, was the oldest fraternity on the University of Tennessee campus, and the oldest existing chapter, Tennessee Pi, of ATO in the country.

That chapter is gone, but not for me, and not for my son who followed me in that chapter.

My time in the College of Communications is over, but not what I was taught there, and not what both my daughter and son who followed me were taught there.

"So here's to you, old Tennessee..."

Bill Haltom and I wrote this book together out of our shared experiences, out of our shared love for the place and the people we met, and out of the understanding that much of who we are and who we have become was as much grounded on The Hill, as in the waters of the Mississippi, on whose banks we were both raised.

The book was Bill's idea. He came up with the title, and when he told me, he had me.

An accomplished attorney, Bill is also a longtime writer, speaker, and contributor to numerous publications, and the prolific author of a number of books. In fact, he may turn out another book on something or other while I'm writing this foreword. He wrote a book on the origins of seersucker, people. Look it up.

I am an adman, copywriter, creative director, owner of ad agencies (I've bellied up two), and creative boutiques (an ad agency where you dump your own waste baskets and very often work in an attic). I am also a columnist and author of a few books myself.

Bill and I are different.

He is the son of a preacher. I am the son of a mechanical engineer. His father was concerned with the ethereal and matters of faith. My father was concerned with absolutes and matters of math.

Bill was student body president at UT. I was a student body.

Bill was on the UT Debate Team. What I was actually majoring in was a subject of debate.

Bill and I knew the administration for entirely different reasons. He met them running for office. I met them in the waiting rooms outside their offices.

We share a place and experience in our hearts. During football season, Bill writes a weekly well-researched and always entertaining missive to people he met at UT, and a few usurpers a bit outside that window like, say, me. While I was writing this foreword, I got five texts and two calls from fellow Volunteers from my time.

Granted, it's football season, but still.

"Our Alma Mater true; "

While we were there back-to-back, Bill and I didn't meet at UT but later, and have become good friends over the years. We can talk about anything and bring each other to tears laughing. Unfortunately, most of the other people at the table are just brought to tears.

But whatever we may be discussing, our UT experience will invariably enter the conversation, and the conversation glows orange.

This book is motivated by that, but also by the timing and circumstances of our university experience.

The late 60s and early 70s were seminal times in our country.

I matriculated just six years after UT President Andy Holt integrated the campus, and that was still very much a work in progress. I was there when the Vietnam War escalated, student deferments ended, and the draft was held. Bill was there when the war was lost, and the U.S. Embassy in Saigon was evacuated from the roof by helicopter.

I was there in 1968 when Martin Luther King was assassinated in our hometown, and I couldn't reach my family because all the lines to

Memphis were taken. In college, when Robert Kennedy was assassinated in the summer. In college, during the meltdown of the Democratic National Convention in Chicago.

There for Kent State. There when Neil Armstrong took that first giant step on the moon. There when Jimi Hendrix struck a chord with us, and Bob Dylan wrote our lyrics. There when *Hair* premiered on Broadway in 1968, and there when I co-directed my fraternity's satirical version of *Hair* and won Carnicus in the spring of 1969.

Bill was there for Watergate, and for Senator Howard Baker's brave representation of his state, his country and his party at the hearings, a model of balanced and principled leadership for a nation.

The young man Bill grew into the attorney and author who would later write "The Other Fellow May Be Right," a book about Senator Baker.

I was there when Tennessee broke the color line in the SEC in the Georgia game my sophomore year. When UT's Lester McLain entered the game in the fourth quarter and caught his first pass, he became the first Black varsity football player in the conference.

Bill was there when Pat Summitt took the helm of the women's basketball program, and changed women's basketball forever. Again, the young man remembered, and later co-authored with Amanda Swanson "Full Court Press: How Pat Summitt, A High School Basketball Player, and a Legal Team Changed the Game."

And Bill was there when "Rocky Top" was adopted. As I said, seminal.

"We pledge in love and harmony..."

Those experiences are here, with sides of Smoky Mountain cheese dogs and food truck hoagies. Those meaningful moments are recorded, along with panty raids and food tray sledding. Games and races are covered, and some completely uncovered.

In other words, we're going to college. And everything is about to change.

NEVER OVER THE HILL

I began, as so many of us begin our memories, with thoughts of my father and that trip across the state into my future.

I said that college began for me much as it did for him, but college changed while I was there, again and again, and reformed, and regrouped along with society.

But the magic of learning, of first-time experiences, of near-misses and solid hits, of the joys and horrors of independence, and of friendships that have, literally, lasted a lifetime – all of that remains and reminds.

I arrived in Knoxville with my father's values and beliefs. I left with my own.

Much has changed, but I can close my eyes and be in section DD on a bright Saturday afternoon in an instant.

"Our loyalty to you."

That will never change.

– Dan Conaway

CONTENTS

Authors 7
Authors' Note 8
Foreword 9

Orientation and Disorientation 21
    Haltom: Truly coming home 23
    Conaway: Will Horney and the Stereotypes 27
    Haltom: Drop and Add, Withdrawals, Incompletes, and
        Pass Interference 33
    Conaway: Pull this, the registration caste system 36
    Haltom: A hairy situation 40
    Conaway: Flash and the Frat Boys 43
    Haltom: Blackacre and tap dancing: a preacher's son
        goes to law school 57

Curricular and Extracurricular 61
    Conaway: Caught from the very beginning, caught for life 63
    Haltom: Presidents, Chancellors, and other powers that be, or were,
        as it were 71
    Conaway: Credit cards, new majors, and major new friends ... 75
    Haltom: Props for Profs 80
    Haltom: Dr. Bass, skeletons under Neyland Stadium, and
        the Body Farm 84
    Conaway: New years and old ones 87
    Haltom: Speeding in a laundry cart, the story unfolds 91
    Conaway: Bonds and toilet seats 95
    Haltom: The nekkid truth about streaking 99
    Haltom: Tray toboggans down the hill 103
    Haltom: Mountaintop experience 106
    Conaway: Final tally: two bruised shins + one slightly sprained ankle
        + one ski instructor + four surprised coeds + one broken ski + one
        entire family = I've been skiing 110

Tasteful and Tasteless **115**
    Conaway: Comfort. Food. 117
    Haltom: Steamed and stuffed 122
    Conaway: Trucks and handlebars 125
    Conaway: Rare Memories 130
    Conaway: Chicken Tossing Days and Dog Dipping Days: the finer
        points of advertising and promotion 133

"It's football time in Tennessee!" **139**
    Haltom: "Give him six!" – Great memories of UT football in the
        sixties and seventies 141
    Conaway: Just another Saturday: rankings, panty raids, German
        Shepherds, and dorm climbing 145
    Haltom: How Ray Mears changed the image of UT, and
        Pat Summitt changed the game forever 152
    Conaway: Moving the chains 157
    Haltom: How 'bout that Burt? 161
    Conaway: Pride of the Fratland Band and Ice Diving 164
    Haltom: Long Live Queen Vince! 171
    Haltom: The Vol Navy: An Orange Cruise... 174

UT, the Musical **177**
    Haltom: The show must go on. And, my friends, it did, and it does....... 179
    Conaway: California Dreaming and The Age of Aquarius 182
    Haltom: Hunter Hills Theatre: Student stars under the stars.................189

Campus Causes and Causation **191**
    Haltom: From Billy Graham and Richard Nixon, to the Knoxville 22,
        and, of course, the snail darter 193
    Conaway: From King to Kent State, change burns in a nation
        under fire 202
    Haltom: The Open-Campus Controversy: free speech on The Hill........211
    Haltom: SGA: Government of the students, by the students,
        and for the students 216

Side Hustles **221**
   Conaway: Building new boxes 223
   Haltom: The Daily Beacon and other write stuff 227
   Conaway: Shooting the moon for gold 230
   Conaway: The competition you've never heard of, and we won
      it all, and I forgot it all 233

VFL and FFL **239**
   Haltom: A Rhodes Scholar, roads scholars, and a host of Volunteers 241
   Conaway: Found, not lost 245
   Conaway: Godspeed, Helen. We were there 251
   Conaway: Hey, Hope, how are you? 255
   Conaway: Life is a song 259

And so, it ends, and so, it begins **263**
   Haltom: A diploma, just the ticket 265
   Conaway: The final trilogy: Marriage, Graduation, the Hall of Fame
      I do, she did, and we still are 268
      String pulling, living with jocks, and Chaucer 274
      Dwight was right, and the Hall of Fame 282

Freshman Dan Conaway, brand new student, brand new pledge, pretty much – brand new.

ORIENTATION

Discovery. Awe. Possibilities.
Endless possibilities.
New people.

Size.

DISORIENTATION

Time and distance management.
Money and resource management.
Laundry. Hoagies. Support.

Size.

*"My years at UT were wonderful.
If UT was Disney World,
I rode every ride."*

TRULY COMING HOME

I first set foot on the beautiful campus of the University of Tennessee in 1956. My first visit to The Hill was not a "campus visit" to determine if I wanted to attend college there. I was only four years old, and I didn't yet know what college was.

I hadn't even made my decision on where I would attend kindergarten.

My father and mother took me to UT to attend my very first college football game. On a cold November Saturday afternoon, we sat in old Shields-Watkins Field under an orange blanket. I didn't understand what all those guys dressed in orange shirts and white pants were doing on the field kicking or throwing an oblong shaped ball and jumping on top of guys in blue shirts.

My father told me that the guys in blue shirts were from Kentucky, and we didn't like them.

I enjoyed every minute of my first UT football game. I loved the noise of the raucous cheering crowd. I loved the band and the halftime show. And I was happy at the end of the game when my father told me that the guys in orange had beaten the guys in blue even though I did not yet understand the difference between winning and losing a football game.

After the game, my father (UT Class of 1948) escorted my mother and me on a walk across the campus. He showed us the residence hall where he had lived, and the buildings where he went to class. He took us to the old Ellis and Ernest Drugstore, that was the unofficial UT student center in those days, and bought me my first Vol shirt. At that moment, orange became my favorite color, and it is still.

NEVER OVER THE HILL

As a four-year-old in a beautiful orange shirt, I did not understand what a college was, but it was clear to me that my father loved the place and had fond memories of his time there. I later learned that he had attended UT on the GI Bill after serving in the Navy in World War II.

While I had no idea what college was, I realized that UT was a beautiful and special place, and I decided then that I wanted to someday return there and experience the place my father loved as if it were a second home.

I also wanted to go to another football game.

14 years later, I literally followed my father's orange footsteps, and enrolled in the University of Tennessee.

I spent the next eight years of my life there. Yes, eight. Five years as an undergraduate and three years in law school. Yes, I know it should only take four years to obtain a bachelor's degree, but I was redshirted one year, and I wasn't even an athlete.

That's my story, and I'm sticking to it.

My co-author, Dan Conaway, refers to this is as the "Five Football Seasons Plan," which he says was very popular in his fraternity.

My years at UT were wonderful. If UT was Disney World, I rode every ride. I met my closest and dearest friends there.
I also met the love of my life, a beautiful coed named Claudia from the booming metropolis of South Pittsburg, not Pennsylvania, but Tennessee. She looked gorgeous in orange, and after over 40 years of marriage, she still does.

I had wonderful professors, a number of whom I remain in touch with to this day.
I attended concerts, plays, lectures, and a lot of great parties that no doubt led to my being redshifted one year.

24

And I attended a few football games.

Just as I walked the campus with my father when I was four years old, I invite you to return to The Hill with me in the pages that follow. I hope that If you are a fellow or sister alum, it will bring back your own fond Orange memories. And even if you attended some lesser institution of higher education like, say, Alabama, I hope you will enjoy a return of sorts to your own campus and similar memories.

Let's call it a homecoming.

– Bill Haltom

*"A month into fall quarter,
Will was failing calculus — he hadn't seen anything on a quiz above a 60.
I was hanging on in engineering science,
with an average somewhere around
a thermostat setting in the summer."*

WILL HORNEY AND THE STEREOTYPES

That sounds like a great name for a 60s band. This one performed solely on the second floor of Reese Hall in the fall of 1967.

When my lifelong friend Pete Bale and I moved in, Will Horney was in the suite right across the hall. We met the first day on campus. He was from Baltimore.

Yes, Horney was his real name, and he was. Well, we all were, but he was an experienced older man, versed in the ways of the world, or so he would have us believe. He knew about women.

As you, gentle reader, are well aware, any man who says that is completely full of it.

Will qualified, but he was funny and entertaining.

While we were freshman, Will was a junior. He'd gone to a small college and played on their golf team. Now, he was going to finish at UT, and he had been encouraged to walk on and try to make the golf team.

He did. As far as I know, he's still swinging out there somewhere.

Will was a member of Kappa Alpha Order, a fraternity founded in 1865 on the campus of Washington and Lee in Lexington, Virginia, then Washington College. They claimed from the beginning to be motivated by the example of Robert E. Lee, and one of their founders had served under him.

When Lee became president of the college, the fraternity claimed him as honorary founder. They made the late general their spiritual leader in their convention of 1923.

NEVER OVER THE HILL

Civil War cannons adorned many of their chapter house lawns including UT's.

Every year when I was in college and in many of the years since, the chapters of Kappa Alpha engaged in a ritual called Old South Week. On some campuses, parades on horseback took place. On all campuses, the members dress in full Confederate regalia, officer uniforms preferred, strap on dress swords, and have parties with dates in hoop skirts.

Mostly, they get hammered, draw the swords, and hoot and holler. What could go wrong?

I'm glad you asked.

When I was a sophomore and had my pin mate, Nora Ballenger, in Knoxville from Memphis for the weekend, Old South Week was in full gallop at the KA house, two houses over from our ATO house.

We were playing bridge in the living room, when the window behind Nora exploded, and all the glass from it and all the windows on the KA side of the house rained into the room.

It seems one of the members stumbled out of the KA house, put two sticks of dynamite in the cannon for fun, lit a homemade fuse, and sat down beside it to see what would happen.

The cannon peeled back like an onion with the explosion. All the windows in the KA house and the SAE house next door blew out, our living room windows blew out, and General Whoever was elevated and promoted through the air and across the street to adorn and dent the hood of some SAE's GTO.

He was, of course, just fine.

That was Will's fraternity. He even had a uniform proudly hanging in his dorm room, brought with him for the occasion on this campus.

On the second day at UT, Will's roommate arrived. He was from Nashville. Leonard Coleman was his name.

Leonard was Black.

Will seemed to turn a bit whiter as they met and shook hands. I'd love to tell you that Pete and I were sophisticated in our welcome of Leonard. Pete was pretty much speechless, but I jumped right in.

"Where did you go to school in Nashville?" I asked, struggling for a conversation starter.

"Pearl," Leonard answered.

"Oh," I said, "Did you play basketball?"

Pete chuckled.

Of course, that's what I said. Pearl was a Black high school; they had won maybe the last four state championships in basketball. Leonard was Black, ergo, he must have played basketball.

"No," he said, and turned to start unpacking. We had obviously bonded immediately.

It got better, it had to get better.

To his credit, Will didn't try and change roommates, or make any waves. Sadly, in 1967, we were surprised to find that we had Black students among us. Oh, they might be in class, but in our dorm?

Pete's and my high school in Memphis had only integrated in our senior year, and then only with a handful of transfer students from a closed school. While UT's president, Andy Holt, had integrated UT in 1961, Knoxville public schools would not fully integrate until 1972.

To his credit, Leonard put up with all of us.

NEVER OVER THE HILL

A month into fall quarter, Will was failing calculus – he hadn't seen anything on a quiz above a 60. I was hanging on in engineering science, with an average somewhere around a thermostat setting in the summer.

Leonard was an engineering major. Leonard and calculus were old friends. Will and calculus were strangers. Leonard knew his way around a slide rule. My slide rule was a torture device.

He offered to help Will. He offered to help me. He didn't have to do either one of those things, and he asked for nothing, although he did have a weakness for something called a hoagie that we had all discovered in the food truck behind the dorm.

By the way, you can't get mustard out of the cracks and creases in a slide rule.

Short version, we made it through to Christmas, surviving both calculus and engineering science.

I'd love to tell you that I became the architect I started out to be, and that Will fell in love with math and went to graduate school.

I became an adman and Will became a golf pro, but we did become friends with Leonard, and unlike me who lost touch with both of them, I found out years later that they remained friends.

Leonard did become an engineer, and graduated in both mechanical and civil engineering.

He didn't play basketball, but he did learn to lag putt.

Reese Hall was two multi-story buildings connected by a two-story building in-between that housed the dorm office, reception area, post office, etc. The office and post office were in a building within a building in the center of the lobby. We were on the second floor at the end of a long, straight hall with an elevator at the far end overlooking the lobby and office.

Of an evening, after determining that the resident monitor (the guy who enforced the rules on the floor, or tried to) was out cold, we would gather in the hall for a couple of rounds of lag putting.

Pete and me against Will and Leonard.

Put a golf ball down at the far end of the carpeted hall, a good 150 feet plus from the other end of the hall by the elevator. Whoever got closest to the railing at the end without going into the lobby below won.

If the resident advisor was home for the weekend, the whole hall might engage in a tournament, among other things.

Will and Leonard under his tutelage were pretty much unbeatable.

Frustrated by that, I stepped up for my final attempt, and for what would be the final attempt for anybody as it turns out. I didn't so much lag my putt as slam my putt to get past their best ball sitting down there pretty close to the rail.

It hadn't even slowed down when it fired past their ball, through the railing, and right through the glass window of the office below, setting off an alarm, and bringing the dorm to life.

Although plenty of balls had gone through the rail and bounced around below, none had so spectacularly arrived in the lobby.

No one turned me in, and Will's putter was retired from dorm life. However, we would all share the story over occasional hamburgers at the student center over the next year or so before Will graduated, and Leonard did co-op assignments off campus.

You learn far more in college than what's presented in a classroom.

– *Dan Conaway*

"To paraphrase Pogo, you had met the enemy, and it had something to do with the square of a hypotenuse triangle. You didn't even know how to play one, much less a square one."

DROP AND ADD, WITHDRAWALS, INCOMPLETES, AND PASS INTERFERENCE

We UT students knew the deadlines. They were critical, as they affected our transcripts.

The first one was the drop deadline. This was the date by which you could drop a course, and there would be no evidence of such on your grade transcript at the end of the quarter.

Let's say you made the mistake at registration of signing up for a class for which you were totally unqualified. You managed to show up for the first day of class in the right building in the right room. But that's the only thing you could ever accomplish in the course.

Once you heard the professor start lecturing ("Let's begin our discussion of the Pythagorean Theorem, blah blah blah…"), you couldn't understand a word he or she said. To paraphrase Pogo, you had met the enemy, and it had something to do with the square of a hypotenuse triangle. You didn't even know how to play one, much less a square one.

Rather than heading for a certain F on your academic transcript, you could head back to the registration office by the Drop Deadline and drop the course. It would simply vanish from your academic record with no fingerprints.

The Drop Deadline occurred very early in the quarter, long before the midterms. If you missed the Drop Deadline, there was a second deadline, the Withdrawal Deadline. You could withdraw from a course by this deadline, but a "W" would appear on your grade transcript at the end of the quarter, and it did not stand for "Wonderful."

NEVER OVER THE HILL

If you missed both the Drop and W deadlines, and for whatever reason could not complete a course, you could try to get an "Incomplete", but only if your professor agreed to it. Your transcript would then reflect "Incomplete" for the course, but in calculating your GPA it would count as an "F" until you completed the course, and your prof gave you a final grade. Of course, I really don't know anything about "Incompletes." That's just what I have been told.

That's my story, and I'm sticking to it. No, I won't show you my transcript.

There was also an Add deadline by which date you could add a course that for whatever reason you had not signed up for at registration.

I only tried to add a course once. It was right after I dropped Pythagorean Theory, and tried to add Football Physics. But the course was full.

– Bill Haltom

"You're about three days in now in your four-year experience, and you're already beginning to understand why it's a five or six-year experience for some."

PULL THIS, THE REGISTRATION CASTE SYSTEM

The Alumni Gym at UT sits halfway up The Hill on the south side, or halfway down, depending on how you look at it. That's only appropriate because what happened in there kept you suspended between happy and unhappy, satisfied and frustrated ... between heaven and hell ... at the beginning of every quarter.

In this gym, you went through a painful exercise called pulling cards to get your classes.

The Alumni Gym – now the Alumni Memorial Building – was all that and a bag of basketballs when it opened in 1932.

There were six gyms in the place, with the main basketball gym seating 3,200 for games and 4,500 for stage performances when the gym floor was used for seating. The stage was 48 feet wide by 24 feet deep, and I had occasion to perform on it twice (more about that elsewhere in these pages).

There was a huge indoor pool, 12 handball courts, locker rooms, offices, a solarium, and maybe a dungeon in there somewhere. The place had that feel by the time I first set foot in it in the fall of 1967, you know, like you would have to drop breadcrumbs to find your way back if you if you wandered off down one of many dimly lit halls.

The last UT men's basketball game in Alumni Gym was in 1958, until the Vols moved to the new Stokely Athletic Center. However, the Lady Vols continued to play in Alumni Gym until 1977, when their relatively new coach, Pat Head Summitt, moved the women out to play in the clouds of Olympia far above mere mortals.

When I first walked through the doors, I was 17, and a freshman. Lost and invisible.

It was a madhouse. Rugby scrums are better organized.

Students milled about the main gym floor everywhere, and tables surrounded the floor with signs hanging from their fronts and glowering people sitting behind them, seemingly daring you to ask them a question.

I think I peed in my pants a little bit.

First, you found the table with the initial letter of your last name, and received your bona fides (you are indeed a student), a sheet of paper that listed the classes you were to take determined by your class (freshman, lowest of the low), your major (architecture, hard, very hard), and the number of hours you should take (12 hours minimum, 18 hours maximum).

I'm actually a little fuzzy on how you knew what classes you had to take. I may have been assigned an advisor before the initiation rites in Alumni Gym, but the memory is still painful, so I might be blocking.

I take that back, I'm definitely blocking. I was terrified.

You had to determine what was required and what was elective, divided by the number of hours in the day, multiplied by the number of hoagies (just discovered) you consumed, subtracted from the number of hours sleep you needed, added to the amount of stress you could take.

Then, you simply went to the table labelled with the broad subject of the class you needed – English, Math, etc. – and you "pulled a card" for your specific class at the time closest to when you wanted to take that class – allowing, of course, for the times already blocked by the classes you've already signed up for, and whether or not that's a Monday, Wednesday, and Friday time, or a Tuesday and Thursday time, and if there's a lab required at some other time.

NEVER OVER THE HILL

Nothing to it. I think there was a table for bus tickets home.

The number of cards corresponded to the number of places in each class at each time. You had to have a card the first time you showed up for the class. When they're gone, they're gone. See you next quarter. Have a nice day.

You got this. The co-ed in front of you is crying. So is the guy in front of her. You're thinking about it.

Seniors pulled cards first, then juniors – and so on – until you got what was left. If seniors, or juniors, or sophomores needed any of the classes you needed, there would be nothing but dust left in those card slots by the time you showed up.

Plus – or minus – depending on how you look at it, there was a kind of lottery system going on as well. You were given a time to show up, the earlier the better. If you got a later time, the pickings would be exceedingly slim.

You're about three days in now in your four-year experience, and you're already beginning to understand why it's a five or six-year experience for some. Or seven.

You're also remembering one of the books you read in high school, "Lord of the Flies."

And you have a small wet spot on the front of your pants.

But you walked into that gym an untried freshman. You walked out of that gym a combat veteran with ideas of just how you'd do it better the next time, how you'd help those around you, and they'd help you, and God help anybody who got in your way.

You walked out of that gym a card-carrying Vol.

*– **Dan Conaway***

"Unfortunately, as it turned out, I did not resemble Mark Spitz. I was the spitting image of Sonny Bono."

A HAIRY SITUATION

When I arrived on the UT Campus in the fall of 1970, I was a clean-cut All-American boy. Hair neatly trimmed above my ears. A smooth baby face. I wore khaki trousers, button down collar shirts, and penny loafers, and to dress up, I topped it off with a blue blazer.

I could have been a member of the Junior Astronauts Club.

But during the course of my undergrad years, my hair grew longer and my face fuzzier, at least above my upper lip.

By my Sophomore year, I was getting just one haircut per quarter. I would get it before I went home for Christmas or Spring break. And even then, it was just a trim. I remember when I got home, the first thing my father would say to me was, "You need a haircut!"

I didn't have the heart to tell him I had just gotten a haircut the day before as I was leaving the campus and heading home.

At the 1972 Summer Olympics, Mark Spitz won seven gold medals. He had long black hair and a beautiful mustache. The UT coeds thought he was gorgeous, and many had posters of him adorning their dorm room wall.

Suddenly every man on campus wanted to look like Mark Spitz and thereby attract gorgeous coeds. I decided to join the Mark Spitz impersonators. During Fall Quarter 1972, I let my hair grow over my ears and stopped shaving in a painfully slow effort to grow a mustache. It took me the entire fall quarter in an effort to make my upper lip resemble Mark Spitz's, but by winter quarter I had long black hair over my ears (helmet hair) and a black strip of fuzz over my upper lip.

Unfortunately, as it turned out, I did not resemble Mark Spitz. I was the spitting image of Sonny Bono.

My wardrobe changed from frat row to poverty chic. Denim shirts, blue jeans, and canvas sneakers instead of khakis, button down collars, and Bass Weejuns.

Bill Haltom, president of the Student Senate

I also occasionally wore colorful tie-dyed tee shirts that often contained a political or social message such as "Save the Snail Darter."

I somehow avoided overalls, although many of my fellow male students wore them. It was not a good look.

Many UT coeds at the time also embraced the poverty chic look, wearing "peasant blouses" and frayed jeans.

By the end of my undergraduate years, the tie dye and poverty chic look was literally fading on campus, replaced by the disco look, including bell bottom trousers, ruffled shirts, and platform shoes. Saturday Night Fever in orange.

I decided to avoid disco attire. Having failed in my effort to resemble Mark Spitz. I wasn't even going to try to look like John Travolta.

– *Bill Haltom*

"Suddenly, a runner appeared, and I'm sure his performance was described by the broadcast team in the booth. They were probably impressed. Not necessarily in a good way, but impressed. I mean nobody could catch this idiot, and a whole lot of security people were trying."

FLASH AND THE FRAT BOYS

Another good name for a band, and this one would have smashed guitars on stage, and trashed their dressing room and hotel suite before leaving town.

We're going to explore some of their biggest hits.

There's a whole lot packed into your freshman year, and a whole lot of it needs to be left behind. But even if you try, the memories will return, and even if they don't, there's always somebody who will bring them up.

Somebody like me.

When you show up on campus, some things are immediately obvious. The place is huge. There are roughly a million of you there, and that's just the line in the dorm cafeteria. The girls are gorgeous. And that's just the girls in the line in the dorm cafeteria.

The first few days, some other things become obvious. Nobody is going to wake you up and make you get up. Nobody is going to pick up that shirt over there, or wash it, or iron it, or give a crap about it. Not to mention your underwear and socks, although a roommate might mention those. Nobody is going make you go to class, or get you there on time. Nobody is going to tell you that you can't eat that – all of it – or drink that – to the very bottom – or smoke that – right down to the roach clip. Nobody is going to tell you not to do that – or that either – or both at the same time.

Somebody is going to come down the hall at two in the morning and ask if anybody wants to – let's just say – strip down, dress in Saran wrap and jump in a fountain. This is the time in your life when that sounds like a pretty good idea, and nobody is going to tell you it's not.

NEVER OVER THE HILL

For the first time in the life of most freshmen, everything is up to you. Everything.

Flash is the embodiment of freshman and sophomore exploration and discovery – not the names of English poets or Impressionist painters, not solving the mysteries in test tubes or long equations, but rather the names of beer and liquor store clerks who will accept an ID done with a Crayon, and the ratio of pure alcohol to grape juice in a trash can that won't prove fatal if consumed for four straight hours.

Juniors and seniors have figured all these things out, and inserted them into their own lexicon of college survival.

Freshmen who don't, who repeat bad decisions, don't become sophomores, at least not in the prescribed time period. Hometowns are full of freshmen like that, home to stay often by Christmas.

Sophomores who don't, who don't adjust their behavior and priorities, find the college road ahead longer and bumpier. Sophomores like that are often sophomores again, if not transfers, if not in the job market and in night school.

When Flash and I started our adventure, drugs had not yet become the escape of choice, much less the combination of drugs and alcohol. For that dubious distinction, Flash and I are both grateful.

In fact, an entire campus and at least two families are grateful. Cheap bad beer and cheap bad bourbon lead to plenty of bad decisions without any further chemical enhancement.

I will not name Flash. He is an actual person, and he appears and is named elsewhere in this book. He, in fact, appears elsewhere in the rest of my life. The events that follow here are all true. Well, true enough. Give me a break. It was more than half a century ago. The frat boy backups to these antics ... in addition to me ... vary according to venue and time. The insanity is fairly constant.

Flash and BankAmericard; a short gig

The first credit card was BankAmericard – now Visa – and it was soon followed by Master Charge – now Mastercard. BankAmericard's maternity was about the same time as Flash and my matriculation at UT.

Flash's dad thought it would be a good idea to give him one of those cards. He could use it for gas for his car, Dad thought, and emergencies, Dad told Flash.

Turns out, Flash discovered, the card was good at Pero's Italian restaurant on Kingston Pike, and the bowling alley behind it. He could use it for the all-you-can-eat Sunday buffet, and the all-night bowling special.

And he could treat the seven of us that jammed into his beat-up VW to both of those things. And 12 or so other pledges that joined us.

Several times.

Turns out the card was good at the beer store just past The Hill and Stinky Creek on Cumberland just east of campus, and at the beer store by the Alcoa Highway overpass on Cumberland just west of campus – not to mention the liquor store next door.

And his lousy ID and that credit card made Flash our pledge class quartermaster.

You can buy books with it, his and mine, and shaving cream, toothpaste, and a steak at Regis on 17th just north of Cumberland. With a loaded baked potato. For ten.

You can buy all of that, and more, in just one billing cycle.

After Dad got the first bill – and, as it happens, the last bill – Flash got a letter. He showed me the envelope with his name written rapidly and angrily at an angle. Even the crooked stamp looked mad. Inside was the letter, but not really a letter, just a note. He showed that to me, too.

"TEAR IT UP," is all it said, in all caps.

We knew what Dad was talking about. The BankAmericard experiment was over.

Flash was done.

Flash plays the Orange Bowl; immortalized on national television

Following a successful season our freshman year, Tennessee was invited to play Oklahoma in the Orange Bowl in Miami.

Fellow pledge Bob Alley – who would later become my best friend and roommate – was from Miami. Actually, he would correct me, he was from Coral Gables, an upscale suburb of Miami. Miami Dolphins quarterback Bob Griese's house backed up to Bob's, and one of Bob's little sisters babysat Griese's kids.

Bob invited anybody coming to the Orange Bowl to stay with him. He didn't tell his parents. He expected two or three.

He got 11, maybe 12 Frat Boys and Flash. Flash drove half of them down in his packed VW – and down – and down – not realizing that Miami is roughly 6,000 miles away, from anywhere, at the southern tip of a state that's about 2,000 miles long.

Counting Bob's guests was tough because they showed up in a couple of waves over a couple of days. They slept all over that house, and one guy slept in the hedge out front the first night.

That's where he fell. He didn't feel a thing.

Bob's mom, nicknamed Momma Irma after this trip, graciously fed all of them, covering the dining room table with snacks and sandwiches that disappeared almost instantly over three days.

Bob's dad, nicknamed Captain Daddy after this trip, took charge of sleeping assignments and rule enforcement. The rules were his. He was a senior pilot for National Airlines. You did not mess with Captain Daddy.

Then there was the game. Tennessee lost, but Flash passed into legend.

And passed out not long after.

At halftime, the Oklahoma band marched sharply out on the field to perform, each in a tall ornate hat, forming a single line and preparing to break into formation.

Suddenly, a runner appeared, and I'm sure his performance was described by the broadcast team in the booth. They were probably impressed. Not necessarily in a good way, but impressed. I mean nobody could catch this idiot, and a whole lot of security people were trying.

The runner went down the line of the band knocking off their hats, almost all of their hats, before he had to climb back into the stands – aided by Tennessee fans in the first row – and disappear into the stadium and into lore.

The legion of those chasing him never laid a hand on him.

However, after the game, everything he'd had to drink that inspired that performance caused him to be unable to stand up on the bus back to a Coral Gables drop-off, and a little old lady laid a hand on him as she offered him her seat, and helped him into it.

Flash was done.

NEVER OVER THE HILL

Flash plays Stokely naked; twice

Stokely Athletic Center is gone now, demolished in 2014, but it was where the Vols played basketball in our day – where I watched Pistol Pete Maravich make shots from the concession stand when we played LSU – where I saw the Little Rascals in concert - where Elvis played four times in the 70s – where Flash played twice in the same night.

You might say he showed his audience everything he had.

Stokely was right across the parking lot from the ATO house. Maybe 80 yards. That would have been a mid-range shot for Pistol Pete.

One Friday night my sophomore year –with the house full of brothers and dates – the staircase door burst open, and Flash came out running.

Buck naked.

As he wove through the stunned spectators and out the front door, I went in hot pursuit with a couple of other guys who had seen Flash, well, flash by. He headed straight for Stokely.

Fortunately, there was no event that night. Unfortunately, the bank of doors facing frat row were open. Flash beat us there and got inside. As we entered, we knew which way to go. Just follow the sound of the screaming security guard.

Flash was doing laps around the court and then up in the seats. The security guard, all 250 pounds of him on a 5'8" frame, was through running after Flash and on the verge of a heart attack. Standing, barely, hands on knees at center court, he was alternating between yelling at Flash and yelling into a walkie talkie.

He was calling for help from everybody. Everybody**.** And everybody came.

Meanwhile, Flash decided he'd had enough fun, and while we were trying to catch him up in the seats, he went back down on the court, blew by the red-faced security guard, and back out the same way he'd come in, followed by us.

Luckily, he went back the way he came, straight across the parking lot, and through the now-gathered and now-cheering crowd on the frat house porch, and into the house. Even the SAEs next door had come outside to cheer our naked runner.

We, now numbering six, were right behind him. And right behind us were four or five campus cop cars pulling up to Stokely and the agitated and exhausted security guard standing outside.

Remember the scene in *Butch Cassidy and the Sundance Kid* when the lawmen pull their guns on the little old man, and he points directly to the brothel across the street where Butch and Sundance are hiding?

Well, of course you do. You saw that movie. Bob Alley and I saw it five times when it came out in 1969, with and without dates, in the Tennessean movie theater on Gay Street.

But I digress. I do that.

Anyway, that's what the security guard did as I glanced back over my shoulder. Illuminated by flashing blue lights, he pointed directly to our house, and I jumped up on the porch and followed Flash inside.

We surrounded him in the living room, convinced him cops were on the way, and got him upstairs and in the shower to see if some cold water could alter his mood and condition. After all, he was already dressed for the shower.

We posted four pledges outside the shower under orders and with grants of immunity to make sure Flash stayed in the shower, and then headed downstairs to lie to the cops.

NEVER OVER THE HILL

We didn't need to worry. Everybody on the porch was already lying to the cops out front. Even the SAEs next door were lying to the cops.

"What naked man?"

"Really? A naked man?"

Sweating and out of breath, I was interviewed.

What naked man? I told them I was sweating and out of breath because I thought somebody had broken into my car and I ran out to the parking lot to check.

I didn't have a car, but I thought the cop was buying it. After all, he was smiling. After all, no cops even went inside.

The cop talking to me was older and senior on the scene. He'd been around. He did a circular motion with his hand and the other cops broke off and headed back to their cars.

He leaned over to me and said, "Son, I get off in a couple of hours. If I head back over here, would you give me some of whatever that guy was drinking?"

He would have been disappointed. He wasn't drinking anything special. Flash had a limit of maybe four beers, or two shots of whiskey, or half a bottle of Pagan Pink Ripple. After that – as you can see – all bets were off,

Most of this narrative, this and the other incidents, are a byproduct of that limit.

Speaking of Flash, as I was discussing things with the cop, Flash and the pledges upstairs were involved in a wrestling match. Naked, soaking wet, soapy men are hard to hold onto. So I'm told.

Just as the cops were leaving and before their taillights passed Stokely, the staircase door burst open – again – and Flash came out running.

Buck naked. Again. And wet this time. Pursued by four pledges. Dressed, but also wet.

They all went out the front door. To more surprised cheers, from our porch and from the SAEs. And this time from the Signa Chis, our neighbors on the other side, who had now come outside to see what was going on.

Flash headed back to Stokely.

The security guard was still outside, watching the cops leave, probably wondering why they didn't have a naked guy cuffed in the car. When he turned around to the sound of the cheers.

Flash was back.

But Flash – now surrounded by four panting but determined pledges – stopped 20 feet in front of the guard and suddenly started doing jumping jacks, throwing water everywhere.

The guard just stared, then turned and walked into Stokely without a word.

Flash and the pledges then walked back to the house, looking like five guys coming back from class. Five wet guys coming back from class. Four dressed and one naked.

Flash bowed to the cheers, and went inside.

Flash was done.

NEVER OVER THE HILL

Flash plays Columbia State Community College;
by invitation of the university

Flash went on tour not long after his full-frontal assault on Stokely. It was a command performance.

You might say it was a combination of things that sent Flash away; the combination of lousy grades, lousy behavior, lousy choices, and the lousy habit of repeating all of that for five consecutive quarters.

Other than that, he was fine.

The university gave him a choice, and a set of conditions. Here was the choice:

Leave, go to Columbia State Community College for a semester, take these courses, make at least a 3.0 grade point average, behave yourself, and return with an official letter and transcript that says you did all that, and we'll give you another chance here. And we'll also watch you like a hawk.

Or just leave.

Flash took door number one.

Flash also had further motivation. His high school sweetheart was also at UT and still with Flash through all of his misadventures. Until now. Even she had had enough.

And another fraternity brother had been waiting in the wings and was now dating her. Fraternity brothers can be jerks just like anybody else.

So, Flash was off to Columbia State Community College in Columbia, Tennessee, an almost brand-new institution started in 1966. Lady Bird Johnson, accompanied by President Lyndon Johnson, officially dedicated the new campus in 1967.

Lady Bird was followed by Flash in 1969.

And he wasn't alone. Another of our fraternity brothers received the same invitation and choice from UT at the same time. He had been caught with a number of others dumpster diving for the mimeograph stencils of the zoology exam and selling copies of the exam to eager students.

Further, our fraternity sweetheart at the time, Julie Dodson, was from Columbia, and could tell them where to get a good hamburger.

We were nothing if not supportive.

Flash was done.

I'll pause here while Flash attends Columbia for a small-world UT story.

In 1995, I was an adult leader on a backpacking trip to Philmont National Scout Ranch outside of Cimarron, New Mexico, in the Sangre de Cristo Mountains. Our son Gaines was with me (UT, 2003).

The exercise involves strapping a 50-pound pack on your pack along with ten or so Boy Scouts, and walking out of base camp. You return 11 days later, having walked up and down from altitudes of 6,000 to 13,000 feet, across 70 to 80 miles of everything the terrain and experience has to offer.

You can go several days without seeing anybody.

One of those days, we were walking up a mountain on a narrow trail single file when our patrol leader for the day saw a group coming down the mountain. Protocol calls for you to give the right of way to those going down, so we stopped, leaned up against the mountain's rock wall, and gave them room.

As they passed, I noticed distinctive Southern accents. Philmont has Scouts and accents from all over the country and the world, but this one sounded like home.

As one of the adults went by, I asked where they were from, "Tennessee," he said. I laughed and said, '"Us, too. Memphis. How about you?" "Columbia," he answered. I laughed again, "The sweetheart of my college fraternity was from Columbia. She was a UT cheerleader named Julie Dodson."

"I live in her house," he said.

And we both howled and almost fell off the mountain – a remote mountain about 1,400 miles away from our common ground. He had bought her parents' house when they moved to a retirement community.

Now, let's catch up with Flash.

Flash has a comeback tour; triumphant and still playing

Flash returned to UT for Winter Quarter of our junior year. He'd met every condition. His grades were up. He'd stopped drinking. And he'd proved himself to his girlfriend, too, and won her back.

They were married while still in college, and they're still married today.

He's been a success as a husband, a father, a church leader, a businessman, a community leader, supporter of UT, and a good friend for more than half a century.

He could have lost it, and he knows it, and the lesson was learned, and a man was made from the pretty raw material of a pretty wild boy.

Flash has an occasional beer. One. I'm lucky because he sometimes has it with me. Make no mistake, I was also lucky to get in on those trips to

Pero's on the BankAmericard.

And by the way, if you're wondering about the other guy – the mimeograph dumpster diver – who joined Flash for the Columbia sabbatical, he came back, too.

He got his degree from UT. And his Masters.

And he's still a friend, too. And still a touch crazy,

– Dan Conaway

*"I kept hearing Eddie Albert and
Eva Gabor singing, 'The chores! The stores!
Fresh air! Times Square!'"*

BLACKACRE AND TAP-DANCING: A PREACHER'S SON GOES TO LAW SCHOOL

In 1975, after just five years as an undergraduate, I obtained my Bachelor of Conservative Arts degree from the University of Tennessee. I had somehow passed 180 quarter hours of coursework and overcome hundreds of dollars in unpaid student parking tickets (See final chapter, "A Diploma, Just The Ticket") to earn my orange and white sheepskin.

But I was not ready to leave The Hill. I had had a fabulous time during my half decade as an undergraduate. I was like Zonker Harris in "Doonesbury", who said about being a college sophomore, "Those were three of the best years of my life."

And so, determined to spend a few more years on The Hill, I applied to law school.

Miraculously, I was accepted. I'm still not sure how that happened. I must have been admitted under Proposition 48, or perhaps the law school admissions committee used one of those butterfly ballots that was later used in Florida to count votes in a presidential election.

In any event, I was admitted to the Big Orange College of Law, and enrolled there in September of 1975. I was probably the greenest, most unprepared student ever admitted to UT Law School.

Several years ago, a newspaper reporter was writing a story about the life of the legendary baseball player, Yogi Berra. The reporter interviewed Yogi's first grade teacher, and asked her whether Yogi was a good student. She replied, "Well, no. Not only did Yogi not know anything, he didn't suspect anything."

NEVER OVER THE HILL

Well, I was the Yogi Berra of my law school class. Not only did I not know anything about law, I didn't suspect anything.

I still vividly remember my very first day of law school and the first class I ever attended. The class was called "Contracts I" and taught by a delightful fellow named Joseph G Cook.

Based on my undergraduate experience, I expected Professor Cook to walk in the classroom, greet us all with a warm smile, and then spend the first class session introducing himself and telling us about the course we would study for the next several weeks.

But instead, Professor Cook walked in the classroom, dropped a huge textbook on the podium, and then glared at the class with all the warmth and happiness of a man who was suffering from a case of terminal hemorrhoids. And then I heard the following words come out of Professor Cook's mouth:

"A offers to sell Blackacre to B for…"

I suddenly went into a panic. I hadn't the slightest idea what the word "Blackacre" meant. I assumed it was some brand of chainsaw.

To my horror, Professor Cook began to call on many of my fellow inmates, or rather classmates, and ask them questions, all involving an A trying to sell something called "Blackacre" to a B.

In desperation, I turned to my buddy, Cliff Knowles, who was sitting beside me. "What in the heck is a Blackacre?" I frantically whispered to Cliff.

Cliff, a Vandy grad who would go on to be editor-in-chief of the law review, calmly replied, "You know, Blackacre. It's like the name of a farm."

Well, of course. Blackacre. Sort of like Green Acres, the farm that the great lawyer Oliver Wendell Douglas bought on that TV show I watched when I was a kid.

Throughout the rest of the class, I set in sheer terror, waiting for friendly Professor Cook to call on me. To make matters worse, during this whole time, the dad-blasted Green Acres theme song kept blaring through my mind.

I kept hearing Eddie Albert and Eva Gabor singing, "The chores! The stores! Fresh air! Times Square!"

After Contracts class ended, I stumbled across the hall to my first Property class, where so help me, a professor by the name of Dr. Overton performed a tap dance routine. I wondered if that was a metaphor for the performance I would be giving over the next three years. Worse yet, I suddenly noticed that among my classmates were several Eddie Haskell-types who kept waving their hands, volunteering to answer the tap-dancing Professor's questions.

These dweebs couldn't wait to use Property law terms like "fee tail" and "executrix" and "seisin." The only way I could use the word "seisin" was to say, "It's football seisin!"

Heck, my fellow law students not only knew what "Blackacre" meant. Their daddies probably owned Blackacre.

I was totally unprepared for this, because as a first-year law student ... a first-minute law student ... I had very little idea what lawyers actually did for a living. There were no lawyers in my family. I come from a long line of preachers. In fact, folks in my family firmly believe that the Lord calls preachers, and the Devil calls lawyers.

Preach.

Consequently, my knowledge of lawyers prior to enrolling in law school in the fall of 1975 was limited to what I picked up watching "The Perry Mason Show" once a week from 1957 to 1966. However, I cannot remember a single episode where either Perry, Hamilton Burger, Della Street, or Paul Drake ever used the word "Blackacre."

NEVER OVER THE HILL

Well, thanks to the good Lord above, I managed to survive not only the first day of law school, but to also stumble through the next three years and somehow obtain my juris doctorate degree.

The power of prayer.

The highest honor a law school graduate can receive is being named to something called "The Order of the Coif." I didn't obtain that honor, but I was named to Order of the Cuff, given to law students who wore the nicest trousers.

Nearly 50 years later, I still suffer from law school post-traumatic stress disorder. I have this recurring dream in which the Dean of the law school calls me and says, "Bill. I'm afraid we have some bad news. It appears there was an error on your transcript for the fall quarter of 1975, and you need to come back and re-take Professor Cook's Contracts class."

I pray this nightmare will never become a reality. But if it does, I intend to be ready. If Professor Cook asks me about Blackacre, I'm going to tell him it's probably the best brand chainsaw money can buy.

Amen.

– Bill Haltom

CURRICULAR

Memorable professors and teachers,
what they professed and taught,
and some memorable lessons.

EXTRACURRICULAR

Memorable events and excursions, and
the unforgettable people who shared them.
It should be noted that many of your parents –
and grandparents – were a lot more interesting
than you might have thought.

NEVER OVER THE HILL

*"Wake up, son. This is Andy Holt,
and we're going fishing"*

CAUGHT FROM THE VERY BEGINNING, CAUGHT FOR LIFE

At nine o'clock on a Monday morning in 1967, the phone in the frat house rang.

The phone was in the cloakroom. Yes, we had a cloakroom, although very few if any of us wore cloaks or even knew what they were. The only other phones were in the office, one phone for the officers – don't you know – and in the housemother's apartment, one phone for her exclusive use, and one on the wall upstairs.

Everybody else – the 48 guys who lived there and the other 104 actives, and any visitors – had to use the wall phone in the cloakroom. That was in order of priority: first, the actives (members); second, the rest of the world; third, and last behind the rest of the world, any of the 52 brand-new pledges. The one upstairs was for actives only. If a pledge used that one, well, you might as well tell whoever was on the other end not to call you anymore. You weren't going to be around.

Somebody answered the phone, and panicked. Somebody else did triage on who was going to get this call, and then they threw me under a UT bus.

I'd been on campus all of a week, I was a lowly pledge, I happened to be in the house doing something lowly when the phone rang.

This call was for me.

"Can you hold for Dr. Holt?" the woman said, her tone professional.

Dr. Holt.

NEVER OVER THE HILL

Andy Holt. He had the physical profile of a 1952 Pontiac Chieftain hood ornament, and the legendary profile of a tireless champion of both public education and educators. He had ears big enough, with a gentle breeze behind them, to push a boat down the Tennessee River, and a vision big enough, with a gentle spirit behind it, to push a university to integrate, to start a Space Institute, to triple student enrollment and double faculty size.

His voice was equal parts molasses and grits, his wit sharp enough to shave with, and his personality warm enough to take the chill out of anybody or any room. He was a speaker and storyteller so mythically gifted; he could open both the minds and wallets of state and federal legislators.

As in Dr. Andrew D. Holt. As in President of the University of Tennessee, calling me, on my frat house phone.

"Yes, uh, ma'am," I said, my voice trembling. I hadn't fully unpacked my footlocker. I still had textbooks to buy. I still hadn't been to a game in Neyland Stadium.

Some, in fact, most of you would wonder what this was about. I, on the other hand, was programmed to wonder what have I done? Why would the master of my as yet unexplored universe want to talk to me?

My trips to the principal's office were never about notable achievement, well, not the noble kind of notable.

I knew though. As the phone was handed to me, one of my fellow pledges said, "I think it's about the banner." He had the farewell-we-barely-knew-ye expression on his face.

The banner. Dr. Holt wanted to talk to whoever was responsible for the banner.

When I pledged ATO, somebody said I had some artistic ability. I really didn't have much, but somebody saw some cartoons I did, so they made me the official sign painter. I was to do a banner for every home game, about 15 or 20 feet wide by a couple high, to hang on the front of the house.

We would be playing Auburn the following Saturday, the first home game of the 1967 season.

I had three choices for a theme since Auburn still can't make up their minds about what to call themselves - Plainsmen, War Eagles, or Tigers.

I chose Tigers, wrote my message, got some other pledges to help, painted the banner, and taped it up on the house the Friday before that Monday.

The voice came on the line. He didn't even ask my name, he just started a story, a story whose end was up to me:

"Son, this is Andy Holt," he drawled, like he was a mere mortal. "Do you know where the administration building is up here on The Hill?"

"Yessir," I said, only vaguely aware of Hill geography.

"Well, the Trustees have assigned me a fine office in this building. View of the whole campus from up here. And, son, we got a lot going on right now. New buildings popping up like daisies on The Hill. Exciting time to be at Tennessee."

"Yessir," trying not to whine.

"The Trustees have also provided a home for my wife and me. Sequoyah Hills. Beautiful. Every morning, I take a different route to The Hill, take my time, so I can take a look at all we're doing. This morning, I came through that brand-new fraternity park – right by your fraternity house, son. Impressive."

"Yessir," trying not to cry.

NEVER OVER THE HILL

"You know, I can just see a corner of fraternity park from my window, across from my desk. Pretty sure I can see your house from here ...," he waited.

"Yessir," I said, wondering if Dad was going to come get me, or would I have to take the bus home after getting thrown off campus.

"I'm going to pour myself another cup of coffee and make my way over to that window. I'm getting old, son, so it's going to take me a bit to get over there .... when I get there, when I take a look out over the campus we should all be proud of ... (pausing)

That banner best be down."

"Yessir," I said, already dropping the phone, which had gone to a dial tone. I grabbed another pledge and ran outside. I got on his shoulders and ripped the banner down.

Here's what the banner said. You might want to cover your children's eyes, you might wonder what I was thinking, you might wonder if I have any respect for women, you surely might.

BEAT THE TIGERS. A LITTLE PUSSY NEVER HURT A VOL.

One of the things that made Andy Holt Andy Holt was his understanding that college students – especially men – are idiots, and that they should be given the opportunity to improve on that condition while under his watch.

There's still hope for me.

At five o'clock on a Sunday morning in 1969, the phone in the frat house rang.

For those of you not familiar with five o'clock on a Sunday morning in a frat house, just think of a graveyard, except that the residents of a graveyard are more likely to be up and about. If the phone rings, it's a wrong number, bad news, or somebody calling for bail money.

This call was for me. "This had better be good," I thought, meaning that the news had better be so bad, the urgency so compelling, that my stumbling down the stairs to the beat of my head would be warranted.

"Daniel? Or is it Danny or Dan?" said the voice. "This is Andy Holt."

Couldn't be. I mean what are the chances of lightening striking twice? I knew this was somebody's idea of a joke.

"Yeah, right," I coughed through the bale of cotton behind my teeth. "Who the hell is this?"

"Wake up, son. This is Andy Holt and we're going fishing. I'll pick you up in 15 minutes."

The fog cleared and I recognized the voice. After all, I had heard it two years before, and this time, he used my name. Thank God, he didn't say nice to talk to you again, or I'm surprised you're still here.

Just my name. And fishing.

Andy Holt made it his business to meet as many students as he could. He would host faculty and students at his house – weekly. He would ferry weary students up The Hill on his way to the office. He wandered the student center grill and had lunch with random students he saw.

And if he already knew your family, he would make it a point to spend some time with you before you graduated.

His administrative assistant had serious mix-and-match skills and some sort of Voodoo-good Rolodex to be able to make connections with Andy across 26,000 students at any given time, and a new batch arriving every quarter.

NEVER OVER THE HILL

During his salad days as a teacher and administrator at the West Tennessee State Teachers College, now the University of Memphis, he became a close friend of both my Godfather, R.M. Robison, the dean of men at then Memphis State, and one of my uncles, the editor of *The Commercial Appeal* in Memphis.

I didn't know that, but Andy Holt did. In fact, that uncle, Frank Ahlgren, was a UT Trustee at the time, and I'm not sure Uncle Frank knew I was on campus, but Andy Holt did.

So, 15 minutes after I hung up the phone, found a pair of jeans in the third pile on the right and made it out onto the porch, he docked a battleship of a Buick out front, threw open the door, handed me a bacon sandwich and set sail for some pond somewhere in west Knoxville.

We sat on the bank of that pond and caught, give or take, three million bream. They were standing in line. We talked about my family, about football, about Vietnam, about girls, about raising chickens and changing majors and the Grateful Dead. We didn't talk about Andy Holt.

And we laughed. A lot.

I did not bring up the banner, nor did he.

Then, in what was already a remarkable morning, he did something even more remarkable.

He drove me back to the house, grabbed the big cooler full of fish, and told me to wake everybody up and meet him in the kitchen. In the next hour or so he taught the 20 or so zombies I was able to raise how to clean fish, how to tell a good story, and how to make an impression that lasts a lifetime.

He wasn't a university president in that kitchen, or the former national president of the NEA or a Columbia Ph.D. He was just Andy from Milan, hanging with some buddies.

That magic morning, when he looked at any one of us, he turned the 25,000 students on campus into one. And everyone in that kitchen supports the university to this day and always will.

We knew Andy Holt. We knew how to clean fish. And we knew every single one of us mattered.

And we tell the story.

– *Dan Conaway*

*"Dean Burchett put the
bust in beer bust."*

PRESIDENTS, CHANCELLORS, AND OTHER POWERS THAT BE, OR WERE, AS IT WERE

Unlike Dan, I never got to go fishing with Dr. Andy Holt. But I did have lunch with Dr. Holt on several occasions at Smokey's Palace in the student center.

Dr. Holt often showed up at Smokey's Palace around noon time, wearing an orange blazer he may have borrowed from Coach Ray Mears.

He would grab a plastic tray (the same ones we used as sleds going down The Hill on snowy days), and would then go down the serving line selecting what he wanted for lunch.

After paying the cashier, he thanked her, calling her by her first name, as he had an uncanny ability to remember names. Okay, she had a nametag, but he still had an uncanny ability to remember names.

He would then carry his tray around the dining room, looking for a table where he could enjoy lunch not by himself but with students. He would walk up to table, smile, and politely ask, "May I join you?"

UT students being very bright, we would always respond, "Yes, please!"

Dr. Holt would then introduce himself, (something powerful people always do), and then would ask questions of everyone at the table. Where are you from? What year are you? What is your major? He always made students he met feel like he was delighted to meet them and thrilled that they had chosen to attend the University of Tennessee. And after he met you, he always remembered your name. Nametag or not.

NEVER OVER THE HILL

He was a beloved figure on campus. Chancellor Jack Reese liked to say that UT's favorite gospel hymn was "In the Garden", featuring the chorus, "Andy walks with me, Andy talks with me, Andy tells me I am his own!"

Speaking of Chancellor Reese, he was a beloved campus figure as well. We students particularly enjoyed his irreverent sense of humor. (See his comment on streaking in the chapter herein on the naked or nekkid truth about the brief or rather brief-less fad.)

He loved making fake announcements at campus events. At one in early December near the end of fall quarter, he announced, "Unfortunately we have had to cancel the University's Christmas pageant this year, as we could not find a cast. We searched the campus diligently and could not find three wise men and a virgin."

At a tumultuous Faculty Senate meeting, he reminded the professors of Henry Kissinger's observation that "the reason university politics is so contentious is that there is so little at stake."

He was an English professor who loved renaissance poetry including the works of John Donne, Christopher Marlowe, and of course, Shakespeare. He was also a poet himself, who wrote and shared poems for students and fellow faculty members. To this day I have a collection of his poems along with a photo of us taken on graduation day.

Through my involvement in student government, I knew and worked with many other university administrators including Vice President (and later UT President) Dr. Joe Johnson, Sammie Lynn Puett (love that name) who was the first female Vice President of UT, Dean of Student Affairs Phil Schurer, and Dean of Student Conduct Charles Burchett, who tried to kick me out of UT for hosting the Hess Hall Beer Bust in 1973.

Dean Burchett put the bust in beer bust.

(Dan wants me to note that before Bill met her, Sammie Lynn Puett had briefly served as Dan's faculty advisor for one of his five majors.)

Fortunately for me, Chancellor Reese bailed me out and kept me in school, although I had to write on a blackboard "I will never again host a beer bust" 500 times. That's very hard to do if you've just been to a beer bust.

I'm just kidding about having to do that 500 times. Couldn't have been more than 200.

With the exception of Dean Burchett, I enjoyed getting to know and work with all these administrators.

– Bill Haltom

"She said, 'Dan, when we die, I hope I go a bit ahead of you. Because, if I'm in line behind you, it's going to be a while.'"

CREDIT CARDS, NEW MAJORS, AND MAJOR NEW FRIENDS

By spring quarter of my sophomore year, I was the credit card guru of UT. Hey, it wasn't my idea, it was Esso's.

If you were born well back into the last millennium, like, say, Bill and me, you would remember when today's Exxon was Esso. It was Standard Oil's brand from the days of the robber barons. Get it? Standard Oil, or S.O., or Esso. It became Exxon in 1972.

We have plenty of robber barons these days, too.

Esso had an idea. They wanted to try credit cards for college students, no questions asked, no credit necessary.

I didn't say it was a good idea.

They recruited people on big college campuses to distribute cards. They put the word out in various ways, college papers, bulletin boards, etc., and I somehow heard about it early and jumped on it.

This was the deal: for every student you signed up for a card, you got 50¢. Believe it or not, 50¢ was still worth something, but Esso was having trouble giving the cards away. In the 60s, cars were not the rule but the exception among students.

My turn for an idea.

I put on the only suit I had, and made appointments with every fraternity on the row to pitch credit cards to their membership at a chapter meeting. I offered each frat a quarter for each one, so they were happy for me to pitch.

I held up the card, and asked how many people had a car. Some hands would go up. Then I said, "Let's turn the card over." I would then point out that the card was good at 10 motels in Knoxville and 16 motels in Gatlinburg, not to mention several fast-food chains. Those logos were on the back of the card.

I couldn't sign them up fast enough.

There are a number of things I'll probably have to answer for at the Pearly Gates. Esso cards might be one. One Sunday waiting to process down the aisle – yes, I serve as a lay eucharistic minister in my Episcopal church – I made some smart-ass comment, and one of the priests turned to me.

She said, "Dan, when we die, I hope I go a bit ahead of you. Because, if I'm in line behind you, it's going to be a while."

Amen.

For my fraternity, the pledge trainer sent the pledges out all over campus hawking cards. For each card, a pledge would get a quarter, and the fraternity would get a dime. You might ask how I got the pledge trainer to do that.

I was the pledge trainer.

Before it was over, and by the time Esso went through several billing cycles and found out what a terrible idea that was, I had moved several thousand Esso credit cards around the UT campus.

In the middle of the effort, I got a message to see the head of the advertising department in the brand-new College of Communications. By this time, I was a journalism major. If you're keeping score at home, that was my fourth major – architecture, art, English, journalism. One of my professors had passed the message along in class.

The department head's name was Dr. Donald Hileman.

When I entered his office, if there was any space that didn't have a pile of paper on it, it had a pile of books on it, and that included the chairs. He was busy moving around his desk, taking from that pile, adding to this pile, and he told me to just push some stuff off one of the chairs and have a seat, and he'd be right with me. Then he said something, I'll always remember:

"I'm in promotion, and the better part of promotion is motion."

Dr. Hileman had heard about Esso, too. He was going to engage his students in the advertising academic fraternity Alpha Delta Sigma – ADS – to raise money by signing up students for the card. The funds would be used to support students with travel costs for internships or competitions.

Everywhere they went, my guys had already been. My name and Esso cards kept showing up.

Dr. Hileman was recruiting me. Not to move cards. He knew that pump was dry for ADS. He wanted me to change my major to advertising. He said I was a natural. I was complimented. And after wandering around the entire University of Tennessee, trying out classrooms in every building but education and agriculture, I was finally home.

I was and would remain an advertising major. I would also join ADS and serve as president my senior year.

Ironically, I would later endow a modest fund at the College of Communications to pay for the very thing that Dr. Hileman was trying to raise money for with those credit cards.

Guilt is powerful.

Shortly after my visit, Dr. Hileman became the first permanent Dean of the College of Communications. After my graduation, he became Don to me, and I was further complimented and honored to be asked to join his first Board of Visitors for the college. I served on that board for more than 30 years.

NEVER OVER THE HILL

The new advertising department head was recruited by Don from Florida State. His name was Richard Joel. Don Hileman made me an advertising major. Dick Joel made me a serious student.

I made friends for a lifetime. Don was taken far too early by a heart attack, but Dick lived into his 90's, and we stayed in touch.

Both men saw promise in me and gave me purpose and a career I truly loved.

You might say I should give proper credit to a credit card.

– Dan Conaway

"The most important thing you must understand about the Theory of Relativity is that it is impossible to understand!"

PROPS FOR PROFS

When Dan's fishing buddy, the great Dr. Andy Holt, became the sixteenth President of the University of Tennessee in 1959, he was asked by a reporter for the Knoxville News Sentinel, "What is your goal for the University as its President?"

Dr. Holt smiled and announced, "I want to build an academic program that will make our football team proud!"

University Historian Dr. Milton Klein described Dr. Holt's leadership as "a burst of energy unsurpassed in the University's history." In the decade of the Sixties, Dr. Holt doubled the size of the faculty and staff, saw the construction of eight new buildings on the Knoxville campus, and secured a fourfold increase in state government funding for the University.

By the time Dan and I arrived on The Hill, there were indeed a faculty and academic programs that made our football team and the entire student body proud.

Here are just a few of the great professors I met and academic programs I experienced.

The first faculty member I met was Professor Norma Cook of the Speech Department. Professor Cook was the coach of the UT Debate team. While our football team did not win any national championships during my years at UT, our debate team won two. The debate team did not run out through a T at the start of debates, and goalposts did not come down after their victories, but they should have.

Dr. Richard Marius taught Western Civ (a required course for all freshmen in those days) to packed classrooms of at least a hundred students.

He was a provocative, outspoken unapologetic liberal, and his class was a great show. Unfortunately, we lost him to Harvard (an accredited university in Massachusetts) in 1978 where he became director of the Harvard

Expository Writing program. But even after he moved to Cambridge, he kept his ties to his native East Tennessee and his Alma Mater, returning to The Hill in the summers to direct an annual writers conference, the Governor's Academy for Teachers of Writing.

Another great Professor I will never forget was Dr. Craven who taught Astronomy.

His lectures were fascinating even though I could not understand anything he taught or said. That was OK because Dr. Craven taught my classmates and me that we could not understand what he was teaching since he also could not understand it, and nobody could!

I will always remember his lecture on the theory of relativity. He walked into the classroom and wrote "$E = MC^2$" on the chalkboard. He then said, "The most important thing you must understand about the Theory of Relativity is that it is impossible to understand!"

He then talked for several minutes about energy and mass and particles of matter and anti-matter and wah wah wah…

To me it all sounded like the incomprehensible voice of the teacher in Charlie Brown cartoons. After a while he paused, looked at all of us in the classroom and asked, "Do you understand this?"

"No!" we all responded in unison.

"Good!" said Dr. Craven, "And you never will!"

What I learned from Dr. Craven was that our universe is one big awesome and mysterious place.

Dr. Paul Pinckney was my faculty advisor. He taught me so much not only in his History classes, but also during lunches and over coffee.

Upon learning that I was a "PK" (preacher's kid), he asked me where religion and faith entered into my life. With the arrogance of a 20-year-old, I responded, "I spent the first 18 years of my life, being hauled off to church several times a week. I have had enough of religion and do not want to be involved in it again!"

Dr. Pinckney scratched his beard, and then calmly responded, "I hear you. But someday you may have a family and children of your own. At that point you may want to do for your children exactly what your parents did for you! Give them something to rebel against!"

Very wise advice that I took to heart years later when I took my children with me to church every Sunday.

My favorite English professor was Dr. Richard Kelly. His specialty was nineteenth century English literature, and he wrote biographies of Lewis Carroll and Graham Greene. He loved Victorian humor. But he loved Mayberry humor even more. He wrote "The Andy Griffith Show," the definitive work on the classic television show starring Andy and Barney and Opie and Aunt Bea. Now that is scholarship!

I had many other wonderful professors at UT including Dr. Charles Reynolds of Religious Studies, Professor Pat Hardin of the College of Law, and Dr. Charles Jackson of the history department.

These and other profs were part of an academic program that made our football team and all of us in the Neyland Stadium student section proud.

It was best summarized in my all-time favorite UT shirt, emblazoned with the words,

"2 Nobel Laureates, 7 Rhodes Scholars, 6 Pulitzer Prizes, 10 Astronauts…and we also play a little football!"

– Bill Haltom

"I am grateful that no one ever told when I was in high school and dreaming of going to UT, that there were bodies under Shields-Watkins Field."

DR. BASS, SKELETONS UNDER NEYLAND STADIUM, AND THE BODY FARM

During my era on The Hill, the best-known professor on campus was Dr. William Bass. He was a nationally renowned anthropologist, and an expert on osteology and human decomposition.

Translation: Skeletons and corpses.

I never took a course taught by Dr. Bass. I should have, but I was afraid his class might take place under Neyland Stadium or at someplace called The Body Farm.

Not long after I arrived as a freshman at UT, I heard that there were limestone caverns under the campus. And I heard there might be bodies in those caverns or under Neyland Stadium.

Both stories turned out to be true.

When the University was building the Thompson Boling basketball arena, they discovered a limestone cavern 30 feet by 20 feet and 15 feet deep under what was to be the southeast corner of the arena.

This required a geological slam dunk to fill the foundation.

There was even a story going around campus that if thousands of fans in Neyland Stadium on, say, the third Saturday in October, began to jump up and down celebrating a Vol touchdown, the stadium might collapse as it would be swallowed up by one of those underground caverns.

That event never materialized, so to speak. But as it turned out, there were indeed skeletons under the stadium, over a thousand in fact. They had been carefully stored there over the years by the UT Anthropology Department after they had been examined by Dr. Bass and other faculty and students assisting in his research.

This could give a whole new meaning to Final Exam.

Dr. Bass eventually moved the human remains to "The Body Farm" (that is actually what they called it), not on the Ag Campus, but in a fenced area in south Knoxville.

In this outdoor forensics lab, Dr. Bass studied how human bodies decompose, providing important information for forensic science.

The bones under Neyland Stadium were mentioned in the 2009 motion picture, "The Blind Side." Academy Award winner Kathy Bates plays a tutor for high school football star Michael Oher, who is considering accepting an athletic scholarship to UT. Bates convinces him to go to her school, Ole Miss, by warning him that there are bodies buried under Neyland.

Author's note: Dan wants me to point out that he went to high school with Kathy Bates in Memphis. Nothing in her demeanor suggested to him that she would stoop so low as to even pretend to recruit for Ole Miss.

I am grateful that no one ever told me when I was in high school and dreaming of going to UT, that there were bodies under Shields-Watkins Field.

However, even had they done so, I doubt I would have gone to Ole Miss. I wanted Rocky Top rather than Hottie Toddy, and would have taken my chances.

– Bill Haltom

"The other cop kept his gun holstered. And Calvin sat on his. You see, as we were pulling over onto the shoulder, Calvin remembered his father's pistol in a case in the glove compartment."

NEW YEARS AND OLD ONES

She sent me a message and decades turned into a weekend.

When the holidays and a new year approach and the light from the current one begins to fade, old years and distant memories often brighten. The dull ones don't.

The cutest girl on Tennessee's campus sent me a message, and that sent me back to Houston for her wedding a lifetime ago, and just about the wildest weekend I've ever spent. Extant.

Calvin picked me after work at my summer job in Memphis. We rolled by his parents' house, parked his p.o.s. car in the driveway, stole his father's Lincoln Continental and drove all night, about 75 miles of it in fog, about two hours of it lost in that fog somewhere around Nacogdoches.

We rented surfboards from a Galveston gas station and watched the sun come up trying to find a wave in still gray water.

That's how the weekend began.

Three days later at three in the morning we were somewhere around Little Rock headed back to Memphis. We'd picked up another passenger for the trip back, KC, and he was driving. Calvin was riding shotgun and I was out cold in the back seat. All four of us were a wreck. The three UT students and the Continental. It was smoking more than my pack-a-day habit at the time, the air conditioning had crapped out, the front end was smashed in from a lost battle in a Houston intersection, and the left rear tire was shakier than we were. KC was about five six, maybe, and wearing a brand-new cowboy hat that was bigger than that.

That's what the Arkansas troopers saw – a smoking, wobbling, smashed ship of a car with out-of-state plates, the windows down, and apparently being driven by a kid in a cowboy hat since that's all they could see above the gunwale of the driver's door.

They pulled us over and one approached down the driver's side, the other down the passenger side, just as I woke up and sat bolt upright in the back seat, surprising both cops, and causing the one I was looking at to point a nickel-plated cannon right between my eyes and suggest that I not move. I didn't, but a number of things inside of me did.

The other cop kept his gun holstered. And Calvin sat on his. You see, as we were pulling over onto the shoulder, Calvin remembered his father's pistol in a case in the glove compartment. Using the kind of late-night logic college students are known for, he decided it would be better to take it out of the glove compartment and hide it somewhere. Where he hid it – sitting on it – was just about exactly where he pulled that idea from originally.

They never saw it, even when we were invited out of the car and Calvin had to leave the nest. One was still suspiciously watching me, the other was suspiciously staring at KC's Arizona license, and both couldn't wait for the story.

We told them that we'd been to a wedding in Houston, that we were on our way home, and pointed out that the rented tuxes in the trunk would back up our story.

"Open the trunk," they said. "You can't make us do that without a warrant," KC the pre-law major said.

One cop pushed his hat up and sighed, and I think I heard the other one cock the cannon.

"That's right, son," hat said, "but if you don't open that trunk, we're going to pile all three of you into that patrol car, go find a judge, and wake him up. If we do that, I can promise you two things. We will get the warrant. And you will spend at least tonight in jail."

"Gospel," said cannon.

"KC," Calvin said, "shut the hell up," and opened the trunk, revealing the tuxes.

They let us go, and that's how the weekend ended.

Space and decorum prohibit a detailed description of what happened in between, but there was a wedding, the statutes have run on everything else, and some of those things – like the Chicken Ranch – will remain the stuff that feeds stories and memories.

None suitable for my grandchildren, at least not yet.

In Charlene's message, she told me she wanted to surprise her husband, Garner – fraternity brother of those in the Continental – with one of my earlier books for Christmas. She included a little family news and ended with "we're still madly in love and still having fun."

It doesn't get better than that.

So, when the next one rolls around, more than just a Happy New Year, allow me to wish you some wild and colorful memories of old ones.

It still surprises me that so many of mine are orange.

– *Dan Conaway*

"Pam stopped screaming and started laughing. The Campus Police Officer didn't."

SPEEDING IN A LAUNDRY CART, THE STORY UNFOLDS

Most UT students are law-abiding citizens. But from time to time even the best students might have a brush with the law.

And besides, this book isn't about most students, and certainly not about the best students.

My brush came one memorable evening when UT Campus Police pulled me over for speeding down Cumberland Avenue.

Actually, I was not pulled over. I ran into a streetlight.

The interesting part of this story is that I was not in a car at the time of my unfortunate accident. I was in a laundry cart that I had, shall we say, borrowed from Clement Residence Hall.

It all started when I was chasing a beautiful coed name Pamela around Clement Hall, and I literally mean around Clement Hall.

At some point I found an empty laundry cart in front of the dorm. I noticed it was on wheels, and I asked Pam if she would like to take a ride with me. To my surprise and delight, she said yes! We then climbed into the cart.

And then there came another surprise. The cart started moving. I look behind the cart and discovered that Pam and I had a driver, or more accurately, a pusher. It was our friend Bill Hickerson who had decided to join in the laundry cart cruise. He didn't climb in the cart. He just started pushing it.

Pam and I assumed Bill would push our cart around or perhaps even through Clement Hall. But the next thing we knew, our cart had left the residence hall courtyard and had actually entered busy Cumberland Avenue that ran alongside the dorm.

NEVER OVER THE HILL

Pam screamed as we headed east through the traffic. I assumed Bill was going to chauffeur us to the Roman Room or some other fine off-campus dining establishment that had a parking for laundry carts. But we built up speed and zoomed past the Roman Room and Sam and Andy's. I looked back to ask Bill to slow us down and pull us over. But Bill was no longer there. He had either let go or lost control of the cart, and we were speeding down the Cumberland strip with no brakes.

Suddenly we came to a hard stop. We had veered off the street and onto the sidewalk where we hit a streetlight.

Pam screamed one last time, as she had screamed throughout the entire brief cruise.

I started to comfort her, when suddenly I noticed flashing blue lights next to our wrecked laundry cart. It was the UT Campus Police who had chased us as if we were Burt Reynolds and Sally Field in "Smokey and the Bandit."

At this point I made my second mistake of the evening, the first having been climbing in the laundry cart with gorgeous Pam. I stood up in the cart with my hands raised over my head and asked, "How fast were we going, Officer?"

Pam stopped screaming and started laughing. The Campus Police Officer didn't.

"Are you crazy?" he asked me. "What are you doing in a laundry cart on Cumberland Avenue…in the traffic????"

"I don't know, Officer," I replied. Nodding toward Pam, I added, "It seemed like a good idea at the time."

I thought I was about to be taken into Campus Police custody and maybe even the Big Orange Jail. But then my laundry cart driver, Bill, arrived, having been in his own chase after he had, shall we say, lost control of the vehicle.

Sounding like Eddie Haskell from the old "Leave It to Beaver" TV show, Bill stepped up the Officer and politely said, "Sir, we were just having some fun riding the cart around our dorm courtyard when it rolled out onto Cumberland! I have been chasing it to pull it and friends here off the road. I am terribly sorry. Please let us push the cart back to the dorm. I will make sure my friends and I return to our separate dorm rooms, finish our evening studies, and go to bed after enjoying a glass of milk!"

At this point the Officer started laughing. "Yes," he said to our chauffeur. "You do that! And don't let me ever see you crazy kids again."

We made it safely back to Clement Hall, pushing the laundry cart along the sidewalk very slowly.

Bill the Laundry Cart driver went on to UT Medical School and became a plastic surgeon, Beautiful Pam went to law school and became a federal judge.

And I never climbed in a laundry cart again.

– *Bill Haltom*

"Or not. Instead, he turned to me and opened with, 'Tell him the toilet seat story.'"

BONDS AND TOILET SEATS

Fraternities get a lot of grief these days and deservedly so. Not just because of the headline-grabbing, racist and criminal behavior of the worst examples both past and present, but because of the nasty rebirth of exclusion that their very nature seems to support.

And there's this: fraternities are comprised of young men and young men do stupid things. They come up with them. They do them. And they pull out their phones and record them.

Stupid.

The difference between now and my days roaming the fetid halls of a fraternity house in the dim reaches of time is simply the phone. Stupid was alive and well. But something else came from those days, more than simply shared experience and space, certainly more than initiation rites and secret handshakes and Greek letters.

Those aren't the bonds that last. You came of age together. You learned together. And some of you, not all but some of you, thrown together by circumstance will remain friends long past stupid into choice, into the whole of your life, into people who are only one phone call, one reminder, one story away from just getting started.

That's the stuff of bonds and toilet seats.

A University of Tennessee fraternity brother invited me to lunch the other day, he said, to share my experience as a columnist with his son, just beginning a career in journalism.

NEVER OVER THE HILL

Or not. Instead, he turned to me and opened with, "Tell him the toilet seat story."

So, I did.

Calvin and I were duty pledges. It was our turn to spend the night at the frat house doing grunt duty – answering the phone (one down, one up), going on mountain runs (getting chili cheese dogs from the Smoky Mountain Market for brothers), answering vital questions (such as the hometown and major of every brother) – and so on.

Being a weeknight and slow, everything was quiet by around two in the morning. Calvin and I had to remain awake, and we spent the time discussing various pranks we might play on these guys while they slept, you know, just theoretical ideas.

So, we stole the toilet seats.

The ten or so from the group heads upstairs. The two from the women's bathroom downstairs, and the one from the men's. The one from the bathroom between the two snoring officers' rooms downstairs. The one from the kitchen bathroom. And, God forgive me, the housemother's bathroom.

Every. Single. One.

Somewhere around 20 in all, draped over his arms and mine like a foul wreath selection, around our necks like nasty horse collars, spirited out the door across the adjoining athletic field all the way to Calvin's dorm room. We actually passed a couple of people who nodded, just saying hello, seeing nothing unusual in this passing potty parade.

We took the back off behind the sink in his room and stored them all in the pipe space between his room and the room next door.

I hid the next day, a Friday, and over the weekend in the obscurity of a 26,000-student campus avoiding the frat house. Calvin blew town and came home to Memphis for the weekend. The fraternity acted like, well, a place with 40-plus people living in it with no toilet seats.

They endured a weekend, and a party, without toilet seats. The housemother went to her sister's and the brothers put out the word, either the toilet seats or Calvin's and my pledge pins by Sunday at 6.

Calvin came back Sunday and while we were trying to figure out how to gracefully return 20 or so toilet seats and not get flushed (okay, that was bad), one of our pledge brothers showed up to give us some news.

The entire pledge class had placed their pledge pins in a bowl in the frat foyer.

Every. Single. One.

Faced with no toilet seats and no pledges, a reprieve was issued. The toilet seats were returned … and reinstalled, I might add, with apologies … and order was restored.

It's funny what really shapes your life.

– Dan Conaway

NEVER OVER THE HILL

"We aren't going to do anything. We are convinced that in a few days this streaking fad is going to peter out."

THE NEKKID TRUTH ABOUT STREAKING

During my years on The Hill, I witnessed and sometimes participated in numerous unofficial and even unauthorized extracurricular activities. These included frisbee tosses, panty raids, beer busts, and dining hall food fights.

But the most memorable extracurricular activity I ever witnessed was a brief fad called streaking.

On a few warm nights during Spring Quarter 1974, several members of the student body (and I mean the student body) decided to take a break from studying, remove all their clothes, and run buck nekkid around the campus.

You will notice that I said these students were nekkid, not naked. I say this remembering what the late great Lewis Grizzard explained was the difference between naked and nekkid: "'Naked' means you don't have any clothes on. 'Nekkid' means you don't have any clothes on, and you're up to somethin'."

I can't recall if the Code of Student Conduct prohibited UT students from running around the campus naked. But nekkid students did get the attention of the fully clothed Dean of Student Conduct, Charles Burchett, but even he was not sure how to stop it.

As I recall, the streakers were first seen in all their nekkid glory one night in the courtyard of the Presidential Complex. It was a beautiful warm night with a full moon. Several full moons, as it turned out.

The first band of streakers were all male, but they quickly won an all-female cheering section from Humes Hall, a female dorm whose residents were known as "the Humes Honeys!"

NEVER OVER THE HILL

News of the streak quickly spread across the campus the following morning, thanks in large measure to the Daily Beacon covering, or rather uncovering the story on its front page, complete with photos that fortunately did not feature full frontal nudity.

At sunset that evening a large crowd gathered in the Presidential Complex for round two. They were not disappointed. There were not only many more streakers, but the field included several nekkid coeds. The news about their appearance soon caused 100 percent of the residents of nearby Hess Hall, an all-male dorm known as "The Zoo", to evacuate the Zoo and join the Humes Honeys in the cheering gallery in Presidential.

Streaking continued for a third night, albeit with a new and bigger location. The nekkid streakers ran to nearly Cumberland Avenue followed by their adoring fans, and began to run up and down what was known as "The Cumberland Strip," and that night it deserved its name.

It soon developed into one of the biggest parties in the history of a University that Playboy Magazine once declared the nation's number one party school.

But just as the non-costume party was really getting going and even the spectators were losing their inhibitions (and in many cases, their pants), the party was joined by several men clothed in blue.

They were Knoxville's finest, police officers, reportedly dispatched by the Mayor to clear the streets of nekkid scholars.

The men in blue frankly had a hard time dispersing the nekkid crowd. I can't recall whether anyone was arrested, although I saw a few streakers mock police officers by raising their hands above their bodies and yelling, "We have nothing to hide!"

The Knoxville media covered it in the first and only X-rated TV news programs in Knoxville history. The Mayor promised the good well-dressed people of Knoxville that the streaking would be brought to an end, so to speak.

But one official who took it all in stride was UT Chancellor Jack Reese. When a reporter asked him what the University was going to do about the nekkid jogging students, Dr. Reese wryly responded, "We aren't going to do anything. We are convinced that in a few days this streaking fad is going to peter out."

Really. He said that.

He was right. But my memories of my nekkid classmates will last forever.

– Bill Haltom

NEVER OVER THE HILL

"You just jumped on an orange tray, lifted your legs, and zoomed down the Hill at speeds similar to Condredge Holloway running down Shields-Watkins Field for a touchdown."

TRAY TOBOGGANS DOWN THE HILL

At halftime at Vol football games when the Pride of the Southland plays the Alma Mater, we sing, "On a hallowed hill in Tennessee like Beacon shining bright."

For me that hill is the one rising above Cumberland Avenue, and the Beacon is the iconic Ayres Hall.

I would like to tell you that my memories of The Hill and Ayres Hall are of classes, conferences with professors, and study groups with my fellow scholars. But the truth is that my fondest memories of Ayres Hall are of sledding down the snow-covered hill on plastic trays "borrowed" from Smokey's Palace, the cafeteria in the student center.

It was the main event in the Big Orange Olympics, and although most of us survived it with just a few bruises, a few did have to be carried on their trays to the infirmary. You know, like Greek and Roman warriors on their shields. (I thought I'd class this up a bit).

It was an icy adventure similar to skiing on the fake snow at nearly Ober Gatlinburg, but you didn't have to rent the trays or stand in lift lines.

You just jumped on an orange tray, lifted your legs, and zoomed down the Hill at speeds similar to Condredge Holloway running down Shields-Watkins Field for a touchdown.

If you managed to stop before heading into the traffic on Cumberland, then you just picked up your tray sled and crawled back to the steps of Ayres Hall to make another run.

It was great fun.

NEVER OVER THE HILL

When Spring Quarter arrived and the snow melted, we would gather on the south lawn of the Hill, in the midst of the daisies (the source of the Vols' color orange), and toss frisbees.

It was not the harrowing icy ride down the hallowed hill, but still great fun particularly if you were joined by Smokey or some other Vol canine who would fetch the soaring frisbees in midair like Lester McClain catching a pass.

And whenever I sing the Alma Mater at halftime in Neyland Stadium, I fondly remember those winter and spring days on The Hill.

As to that orange tray still missing, I know nothing about that.

– Bill Haltom

"I've always suspected the snow-making machines at Gatlinburg were the same machines the 7 Eleven Stores use to make Slurpees."

MOUNTAINTOP EXPERIENCES

One of the greatest things about being a UT student is that it is only about an hour's drive from the campus to the Great Smoky Mountains.

There you can hike, go white water rafting, visit tacky stores in Gatlinburg, or educational museums such as Ripley's Believe It Or Not, and even go snow skiing, although on most winter days at the Gatlinburg ski resort ("Ober Gatlinburg"), it was *ice* skiing rather than *snow* skiing.

There are wonderful hiking trails in the Smokies such as the Chimney Tops where you can reach an elevation of nearly 5,000 feet without the assistance of a Sherpa or a mountain goat, and enjoy a magnificent 360-degree view.

The trail to Mt. Le Conte is more strenuous, and takes you to over 6,500 feet. The Mt. Le Conte Lodge awaits you at the summit, and you can find a rustic room there if you make reservations two years in advance.

Somewhat ironically, one of the easiest trails is one to the highest peak in Tennessee, Clingman's Dome, because it's not a trail at all, but a concrete sidewalk from a parking lot up a ramp to the peak.

And if you didn't feel like an orange Edmund Hillary and did not wish to climb up a trail even if it was there, you could visit Cade's Cove, a beautiful valley at the base of the mountains, and a great place for easy hikes and memorable picnics with mountains for a backdrop.

The only risk on these hikes was that along the way, you might encounter a resident of the mountains, namely a bear. I encountered a few on my hikes over the years, but fortunately there was always a good distance between Smokey and me. No close encounters of the furry kind.

And then, as previously mentioned, there was snow skiing in Ober Gatlinburg, a winter resort that will never host the Olympics, although combined with the tray sledding on The Hill, it could be a nice albeit warm venue.

Skiing at Gatlinburg was a real challenge I'm not sure even Jean-Claude Killy could master.

First, on most winter days in Gatlinburg, you did not traverse the Smokey Mountain slopes on real snow. You were on fake snow manufactured by snow-making machines. I've always suspected the snow-making machines at Gatlinburg were the same machines the 7 Eleven Stores use to make Slurpees.

In fact, if you fell on one of your runs at Ober Gatlinburg (as I often did) and got a mouthful of "snow", it tasted like an unflavored Slurpee. They should have put some syrup in those snow-making machines so you could enjoy a raspberry run.

Forgive me, of course I meant an orange-flavored run.

And the other challenge of skiing the Slurpee slopes at Gatlinburg was dodging obstacles all over the runs ... not trees or rocks but other skiers!

On any given mild day during the Winter Quarter, hundreds of UT students cut classes, headed for Gatlinburg, rented skis and lift tickets, and headed for the icy slopes without worrying about taking a ski lesson.

Consequently, the slopes were covered with bodies of UT students who had fallen and almost drowned in the world's largest Slurpee. And even accomplished skiers had trouble getting on the slopes to begin with as there were bodies blocking the lift lines.

The UT students trying to ski for the first time and had just fallen off their lift chairs on take-off.

NEVER OVER THE HILL

But the nicest mountaintop experiences for me and many of my fellow UT students occurred not during winter quarter, but during the fall when the Smokies were a veritable rainbow of leaves (many of them appropriately orange) and during the stunningly beautiful green spring days.

– Bill Haltom

"My shins slammed into the raised pipe spitting out fake snow along the edge of the slope. Both skis released, and I flipped into the forest like a huge windblown pinecone."

FINAL TALLY: TWO BRUISED SHINS + ONE SLIGHTLY SPRAINED ANKLE + ONE SKI INSTRUCTOR + FOUR SURPRISED COEDS + ONE BROKEN SKI + ONE ENTIRE FAMILY + ONE RIDE IN THE AMBULANCE SLED = I'VE BEEN SKIING

Bill's memories about Ober Gatlinburg – about as real a ski resort as the Swiss chalets on the way down to Gatlinburg were Swiss – brought back memories of my own.

Of just one day, one day that would understandably explain why I don't ski, one day when I spectacularly didn't ski.

Bill's right. It is beautiful up in the Smokies. Even at ground level, as in mouthfuls of ground level.

We piled into a car one Friday in Winter Quarter to "go skiing." Six guys, five of whom had been skiing. In Gatlinburg. And in Colorado for three of them, and in Utah for two of them.

And not at all anywhere for one of them. Yep. Me.

An hour or so later – door-to-door from frat house to Ober Gatlinburg's ski lodge – we piled out, rented skis and poles, bought lift tickets, and headed out to the slopes. I was given all the instruction you receive when you rent shoes and grab a ball off the rack at a bowling alley.

"Ober" is German, perhaps Swiss, for "over," as in "it's over, you're done," and I think also for "this is going to hurt."

The other guys headed for the ski lift to the vast array of slopes, maybe three. I wandered out to the "bunny slope" where I was assured people awaited to give me a clue about skiing. I was 19, the old man on the bunny slope. The instructor was 16, my fellow students were between six and maybe eight.

We were all cutting school, I just wasn't with my parents.

I learned how to put on my skis, how to "snowplow" – forming a V-shaped wedge, bringing your skis together at the front in order to slow down, and "tapping" the inside ski, by raising it and bringing it down to help in a turn. Total time for all of this, maybe 20 minutes. I was ready. I snuck away as the 16-year-old was dealing with a fight between two of the kids over a hat.

I had spotted the college guys' dream; the slope right outside the ski lodge to the left. It was straight down, no turns, no subtleties, and as steep as the ski rental fee. Evidently, one just sat down one's skis to see how fast one could go straight down, and spin to a stop right below the big window of the ski lounge one story up. At least, that's what they seemed to be doing, even racing each other. I say guys, because girls are too smart for crap like that.

I jumped on the ski lift, trying to look natural in an ATO hoodie, blue jeans, Doug Dickey Power T baseball cap, and borrowed gumboots while everybody else was actually dressed to, well, ski.

We got to the top and I waited for the lift to stop. It didn't stop.

I fell out of the lift chair trying to get off and slid about ten feet sideways. I would do that again later.

I made my way to the straight-down suicide slope. It looked much higher from up there. Steeper, too, like the end of the high-diving board. I sat down on my skis, tucked my poles, and eased off the edge.

NEVER OVER THE HILL

Remember the scene from *Christmas Vacation* where Chevy Chase sprays the bottom of the metal bowl with "food additive," sits down on it, and pushes off?

As Cousin Eddie said, "Bingo."

I think I broke the sound barrier, and when I hit bottom, I realized you can't "snowplow" sitting down. As I passed the lodge, I rolled on my side and tried to stick my skis in the air, and took out an entire family crossing my path from the lodge – mom and dad first, the two kids next, and all of us into a snowbank. If that snowbank hadn't been there, I think we would have all ended up in a pancake house somewhere down below.

Nobody hurt. Dad was livid, the kids were laughing, and mom covered for me as I made my escape across the bunny slope yelling my apologies.

Back to the ski lift.

I had a seatmate this time, so, being the gentleman, I let her exit first, and fell again trying to look cool stepping off.

I struggled upright, and wiggle-walked my skis to another slope. It was wide, full of people, and took a right turn back toward the lodge down there somewhere. Looked doable. But doable would have to wait a minute.

As I pushed off, I was crooked, and I veered left into the treeline. My shins slammed into the raised pipe spitting out fake snow along the edge of the slope. Both skis released, and I flipped into the forest like a huge windblown pinecone.

I sat back up, leaned against the pipe, slipped back into my skis. and eased out onto the slope.

I was, in my opinion, doing fine, wiggling a little from left to right, snowplowing like a pro in a Buffalo blizzard, when suddenly in front of me appeared a ski lesson in progress.

The instructor looked perfect, wraparound mirror sunglasses, orange and white knit cap fitted just so, "Instructor" sewn on his ski jacket, not a flake of fake snow anywhere on the outfit, four coeds hanging on his every word as they stood just below him on the slope.

I couldn't stop and I couldn't turn. I was screaming. The coeds were screaming. They saw me.

He finally turned, gleaming smile in place, just as I wiped him out. I spread him around that mountain like linebacker Jack "Hacksaw" Reynolds blitzing a quarterback untouched.

Amazingly, we missed all the coeds as we went by, and ended up in a pile somewhere below. I begged forgiveness, and probably only survived because I found and returned the sunglasses.

My time as a skier was almost over, but not quite.

I got going again and reached the turn in the slope I mentioned earlier. It was just there, just to the right, and I was utterly incapable of turning. I tried snowplowing – again. I leaned. I tipped one ski, the inside ski.

And sped right through and off the course on one ski. That ski caught in the jagged debris of icy snow, ice, and even some rocks. It popped off. I brought the other ski down, and it caught in the debris. Rather than releasing, it broke. Clean in two.

I'm told it's extremely difficult to break a fiberglass ski. Not for me. Not this day.

I decided that was plenty, and my ankle was on fire, so I lay there in the debris field on my half ski and waited for help. I was directly under the ski lift, and from the expressions on the passengers' faces looking down, the situation must have looked dire.

NEVER OVER THE HILL

They brought the ambulance – a golf cart on runners, complete with a flashing red light – and slid me back to the lodge infirmary. No breaks. Some ankle tape. And some crutches. I really didn't need the crutches, but they brought the proper amount of sympathy upstairs in the lodge lounge.

I didn't have to buy a beer for the rest of the afternoon waiting for my friends to finish, comfortably propped up in front of the window watching the suicide slope races.

In fact, and best of all, the coeds from the slope lesson bought a round.

Skiing? Check. Did that in college.

– Dan Conaway

TASTEFUL

The places and choices that nourished us,
say, the Smoky Mountain Market.

We went for good, not good for you.

TASTELESS

The places and choices that might have killed us.
say, Brother Jack's and Fountain City bowling machines.

We tried risky, because safe is seldom fun.

"When somebody yelled 'Hit me, Sarge,' Brother Jack would cackle over by the popcorn rotisserie."

COMFORT. FOOD.

When I went off to college to the University of Tennessee, I was braced for change.

I knew I would have to figure out how to do laundry. And that no one was going to wake me up and make sure I got my butt to class, or tell me to do my homework, or to eat more vegetables. And that the last thing I wanted to do was call my father and tell him I needed more money – he'd made that abundantly clear.

But I knew I'd still have what I'd always had to get me through tough spots, to look forward to even in the stress of the moment, to restore order in chaos.

I'd always have barbecue.

In all the vast experience of my 17 years, wherever I was in the city and in the world I roamed, barbecue was never more than three blocks away. Some better than others, but all good, all close, all comforting. That would be the case where I was going.

Wrong. Like so many assumptions about college, so very wrong.

Even though it's in my state, Knoxville doesn't know any more about barbecue than a pig knows about Sunday. Then and now.
However, there were a couple of places that provided affordable consolation in greasy bags, personality unavailable in the chain choices, taste unavailable on The Strip below the campus.

During the time of Covid-19, our memories surfaced, bringing us together in our time apart, reminding us of each other, and of the things and times we shared in our time together.

NEVER OVER THE HILL

During that dreadful pause, several friends sent me messages independent of each other, and photos, of those two places that we shared a half century ago – places for comfort food.

One was on University, just a mile or so from campus, but much further in experience and circumstance, the other side of the interstate, the other side of town. By day, the building was shared space between a small grocery and fish market on one side, and a meat market on the other – but I was never there by day.

By night – or very early in the morning depending on what two or three a.m. is to you – the meat market side was Brother Jack's.

There was pork in there, and hot sauce, and the warmth it brings. It also looked like frat row in there – no women while dorms had hours, and only the bravest of dates after hours were lifted, willing to face the fare.

What I remember, and the visits are as fuzzy as I was at the time, Brother Jack sat in the corner on a stool next to a popcorn machine converted to rotisserie. God-knows-what was turning in there, and he was basting it. His son-in-law, Sarge, manned the counter in his army sergeant uniform jacket. There were ribs, but ribs weren't the main fare for this bunch.

The frat boys wanted pig burgers – supposedly meat cut from the backs of slabs of ribs, ground, pressed into patties by hand, seasoned, cooked on a flat top, disturbingly white even after being cooked, and served between two pieces of marshmallow bread ... think Wonder. I think they were a quarter.

We stood packing the small place and overflowing outside, there were no seats, and imploring, "Hit me, Sarge." That meant to douse your pig burger with their hot sauce, a nuclear concoction that set your tongue on fire and melted the roof of your mouth.

When somebody yelled "Hit me, Sarge," Brother Jack would cackle over by the popcorn rotisserie.

The hangover cure value of pig burgers was based on that sauce. You were so busy dealing with the aftermath of eating them, you forgot your headache.

The other place was the Smoky Mountain Market – or the Smoky Mtn. Market as the pole sign said – or the Smoky Mt. Market as the sign on the front said. It was a convenience store on Chapman Highway just across the Tennessee River, but the convenience was the food.

There were hot dogs in there. Better yet, there were Smoky Mountain Market Chili Cheese Dogs in there. Two dogs, split and grilled crispy black on the bottom, slapped on a hot dog bun open face, covered with chili, mustard, onions and a couple of squares of sliced American, and then topped with another hot dog bun. Damn. Then there was the Full House. Take a big Styrofoam cup, stand two tamales up inside end-to-end, and fill it with chopped onions, grated cheese, and chili. OMG.

Most of the times when I'd visit, weeknights around 10 or 11 on a study break or a what-the-hell, why-not break, the guy running the counter crew was named Red, skinny and about five-five, the styled eponymous hair about six inches of that. I used to order milk just to hear him scream out, "Pint-a-white!" The scream was so the guy on the covered porch out front where the cooler was could hear him. When he had the milk, he'd scream back, "Pint-a-white!", and toss the pint carton 20 feet through the open window to Red.

We remember the food, and what it meant to us.

I'm going to remember Elwood's Shack here in Memphis feeding the health care workers during Covid, and the Salvation Army feeding the homeless with food bought from local restaurants.

I'm going to remember that each takeout entrée I bought from a restaurant called Mortimer's came with a roll of toilet paper, and every takeout package I bought from a restaurant called Huey's came with a handwritten message of thanks and good wishes from the staff styled on the top.

And there's still barbecue every three blocks or so.

You and I will both remember the unforgettable, those who served us in the pandemic, and at UT, and others through all of our lives. And the warmth from all of it.

Remember them when you tip for takeout, and when you tip period.

Comfort. Food.

As they say, you are what you eat. So, hit me, Sarge.

– Dan Conaway

"There were three diners on The Strip that offered wonderful hoagies. And believe it or not, they were all under one roof, and connected, literally."

STEAMED AND STUFFED

And then, there were the Hoagies. Not just a sandwich. A big long thick feast on soft or crusty bread stuffed with your choice of meat and cheese, and then steamed.

Yes, steamed.

The hoagie was a unique Knoxville delicacy. As least unique to us from west Tennessee. My hometown of Memphis is the barbecue capital of the world, but Knoxville introduced me to the world of hoagies. The sandwich originated in Philadelphia. I understand that's a city in Pennsylvania that also gave us the Philly Cheesesteak sandwich.

Oh, and the Declaration of Independence.

We didn't know from Philadelphia, and you couldn't find decent barbecue in town, but you could find hoagies all over Knoxville.

The best and most convenient to hungry UT students were located on Cumberland Avenue, a/k/a "The Strip." There were three diners on The Strip that offered wonderful hoagies. And believe it or not, they were all under one roof, and connected, literally. They were The Roman Room, Sam and Andy's Tennessean, and Sam and Andy's Deli.

George Captain ("The Captain") owned all three fine dining establishments. I understand he was a nephew of either Sam or Andy. The Captains were a family of Greek immigrants. They loved America, Knoxville, and UT, and they gave us steamed hoagies.

You could sit at the bar in The Roman Room and share a pitcher of beer with your fellow scholars, or you could dine on Formica top table in the Tennessean, or stand in line at the Deli and order your hoagies to go.

You knew you were in the right place because students were in front of the deli eating their hot hoagies right out of the aluminum foil wrapping.

And your orders were custom-made. "I'll have ham and mozzarella on long dark hot!" you would say to The Captain or one of the other Greek immigrants running the deli. And then you would smell your wonderful hoagie as it was steamed in a Fresh-A-Matic steamer.

The "Freshman 15" is the 15 pounds gained by your typical college freshman. I gained all my 15 by eating Hoagies at Sam and Andy's.

– Bill Haltom

"He sat up front at the cash register and took the money. He had a terrific, waxed handlebar mustache."

TRUCKS AND HANDLEBARS

Bill's mouthwatering memories of hoagies brought back some of my own.

Like so many things during his and my back-to-back years at UT, even hoagies evolved. My first experience with the giant sandwiches was in the alley behind Reese Hall. These days, there are food trucks serving virtually everything and as common as jaywalking everywhere in town.

But in the fall of 1967 the truck parked right behind my dorm was an innovation as new and as welcome as the massive sandwiches they made inside the rolling kitchen.

These weren't steamed, but they had basically everything in that truck on what looked like a whole loaf of bread when I hauled my first one up to my room.

When my roommate Pete saw it, he didn't even say anything on his way by me to get one. Between us, I believe we had 700,000 of them our freshman year.

We were on a food plan, and could eat all we wanted at the complex cafeteria. Problem was, we didn't want it, and it wasn't open when we were studying late at night. The light of the food truck was out there in the dark beckoning, the oracle of sliced meat, your choice of cheese.

The name of the food truck was Sam and Andy's.

So, I was a huge fan of Sam and Andy world as well before I was ever in either the Roman Room or the adjoining Tennessean restaurant. The deli hadn't shown up yet.

NEVER OVER THE HILL

The Roman Room had a loose attitude about IDs and the cheap pitchers of beer Bill alluded to, probably PBR, but the price was the attraction. The low quality of the light in there was kind of a low voltage orange fluorescent haze any time of day or night.

I'm pretty sure we wouldn't really want to see what was on those paneled walls, or the cracked floor, or certainly what was under any of those booths.

In the Tennessean, they served the best deal on The Strip – the Vol Burger. I can't remember what the price was, but it was cheap. The patty was the size of a salad plate, thin but huge. It was a smash burger before its time, made fresh and pressed on a flattop grill. It was a cheeseburger with everything, served surrounded by approximately 500 long thin fries.

Greek Sam, or maybe Greek Andy, I can't remember which, was still around and in charge during my time. He sat up front at the cash register and took the money. He had an impressive, waxed handlebar mustache.

He never smiled.

I'm going to give special mention to a dive across the side street beside Sam and Andy's. It was called the Vol Market. It was a convenience store with everything for campus life survival from No Doze to toilet plungers, and a pretty good egg and mystery meat sandwich for a quarter. A fried egg, chipped ham (sure it was), cheese (probably Velveeta), on toasted Wonder bread.

They also cashed checks for a fee, but I don't know why. This is where I first learned about what lousy credit risks college students were. (See my story about Esso credit cards. Esso should have gone in the Vol Market for an egg sandwich.)

The entire wall behind the checkout counter – side-to-side, floor to ceiling – was papered with returned bad checks. The owner put them up there under the heading "Liars and Cheats" for everyone to see.

The Deli behind Sam and Andy's opened my sophomore year, and Bill is right. Steamed is the way to go. Sam/Andy moved back there, too, and manned the cash register. One or both or all the nephews took over later.

Still had the mustache. Still didn't smile.

But that steamed sandwich changed lives.

My friend Larry Busby graduated a year before me at our high school, and came to UT. He was an SAE next door to me at the ATO house. We recovered. We go to the same church now.

Larry fell head over heels for the steamed sandwich. He took the idea and the steamer back home to Memphis and opened the Front Street Deli with his late brother Lee. They had a location downtown that was seen in the film "The Firm" and another near the airport.

Larry successfully introduced the steamed hoagie to a whole lot of passengers while catering private plane companies, and a whole lot of FedEx pilots have "Absolutely. Positively." had to have one.

He didn't have a mustache. He smiles a lot.

In fact, he smiled recently when telling me a story about a legendary late-night feeding trough – Brother Jack's – that I described in an earlier account in this book.

One of Larry's fraternity brothers – Billy Plyler – called the SAE house late one night and asked for Larry. There was a huge rainstorm raging outside.

"Busby, you got to come get me. I was coming back from Brother Jack's, and I slid off the road," he said, sounding like he might have done that even if it wasn't raining. "I took out a wall and ended up inside some kind of variety and clothing store. They handed me this phone through the car window."

NEVER OVER THE HILL

"Oh my God, Billy," Larry said, "Where are you?"

"In the 42 longs," he answered.

Billy was rescued from the 42 longs, and he and two other SAEs – Charlie Rogers and Paul Dorman – grabbed the Memphis-area franchise rights to a new fast-food start-up named after the founder's daughter.

Wendy's.

The Wendy's they opened on Union Avenue in Memphis in the early 70s was number one in volume for the whole company for a number of years.

For them, that was exactly where the beef was.

– Dan Conaway

"And this is where you'll return, where you'll meet your friends, where you'll tell the same stories over the same steaks, where you'll laugh and holler and cut up."

RARE MEMORIES

On other campuses there may be places where special occasions are marked, perhaps some campus feature or structure, maybe a tower of some kind, a fountain, a statue.

You know, I asked her to marry me in front of ... my parents celebrated my graduation in this photo in front of ...

Not here.

If it matters, you celebrate it at Ye Old Steak House. It opened in Knoxville about the same time as I did, 1968.
You'll cross the river and head out Chapman Highway toward Gatlinburg. It'll be on the left, right up against the highway.

The place looks like Davy Crockett lived here. It's a huge ramshackle log cabin built into the side of a mountain – well, maybe not a mountain, but close enough – because your car has to climb the mountain to park behind and above the restaurant, and you'll scale the mountain after dinner to find your car.
You know it'll be packed after a football game. You know fans of both teams will fill it to the exposed rafters. The big open room with the two-story log posts, the mismatched wooden tables, and ladder-back chairs. The back room. The upstairs dining rooms.

You're still going. You'll sign in. You'll buy beer for everybody and bring the long neck bottles outside to wait.
If you're going to impress a date, this is the spot. If your parents visit, this is where you'll ask them to take you.
And this is where you'll return, where you'll meet your friends, where you'll tell the same stories over the same steaks, where you'll laugh and holler and cut up.

The menu hasn't changed much. Big steaks, big slabs of prime rib, charbroiled shrimp with drawn butter. Grilled mushrooms. Baked potatoes. Sweet potatoes. Hand-cut fries. Onion rings. They're cooking the steaks over in the corner where the smoke is, searing them in big skillets and finishing them on the charcoal grill.

The place smells just like you'd imagine, and your mouth waters, hell, your eyes water.

They don't sell wine or liquor, just beer, but you can bring your own.

In our day, we did it right, We brought wine. Both kinds. Mateus, in the distinctive wide brown bottle, and Lancers, in the distinctive tall clay brown bottle – both bottles to become candle holders in two hundred student apartments.

There were other wines available with our fake ID's, but the bottles weren't cool. We knew what mattered, and never mind that either rosé was a lousy choice with a good steak.

As we returned over the years, we brought better wine, and the memories, like the wine, grew better with age.

Then we became the parents, and we were treating our kids and their friends.

And when our daughter got married on a mountain in Gatlinburg, we drove down the mountain to celebrate at Ye Olde Steak House.

Other places are fancier, more sophisticated. None come with the last 50-plus years as a side dish like this one does.

Put my name on the list.

– **Dan Conaway**

"People will come out from all of the hills, coves, and hollers, bring all their dogs, and buy all your groceries, Cas assured us, and that's not all. People would walk their mules and horses in there, get in with them, and splash the toxic stew all over them."

CHICKEN TOSSING DAYS AND DOG DIPPING DAYS: THE FINER POINTS OF ADVERTISING AND PROMOTION

My senior year, I was the president of ADS, an academic advertising fraternity in the College of Communications. One of our responsibilities was coming up with a program featuring a distinguished advertising professional live in our auditorium.

I invited Cas Walker.

So much for distinguished. Almost so much for me. The faculty – as in plural – were not impressed with my choice.

Cas Walker was a grocer, a promoter, a broadcaster, a politician, a con-man, and a character.

He started with one grocery store in 1924, and by the time I arrived on campus in 1967, he had 27 stores, and a substantial finger in a number of other pies.

He started a radio program in Knoxville, the *Farm and Home Hour*, in 1929, morphed it into television, and had it on the air until 1983. He's given credit for helping launch a number of stars, including the Everly Brothers and Dolly Parton. Dolly's first television performance was on Walker's show. She was 10.

He was twice mayor of Knoxville – for a few weeks before being recalled in 1946, and appointed briefly in 1959 in an interim capacity. He served on the Knoxville City Council for 30 years.

NEVER OVER THE HILL

George Dempster – inventor of the Dempster Dumpster – was first a political mentor to Walker and later a rival, had this to say, "If I ordered a whole carload of SOB's and they just sent Cas, I'd sign for the shipment."

Cas once made *Life* magazine in a photograph featuring him about to punch a fellow councilman.

He did his own commercials for his grocery stores, and it seemed he was in every commercial break on all three Knoxville stations. Cas was everywhere. He would often stand next to an easel with handwritten pricing on boards. When he was through with one, he would throw it on the floor to reveal the next one.

I would adopt a variation of that technique in presentations for the rest of my career.

And I swear he wore the same bad blue suit for all of that, at least it looked it. Like he put it on in 1924 to open his first Cas Walker Super Market (two words) and never took it off. The suit went well with his wispy white hair and big glasses. His nouns and verbs not only didn't agree, they fought with each other. His East Tennessee twang rang in your ears long after he was through talking, and he was widely imitated across campus.

He was a huge hit in our packed auditorium. The perfect example of what not to do, of a step too far, of a leap too far.

Of too far in a bad suit.

He wasn't in denial about his outrageous business practices and politics, he knew they were outrageous, and he was proud of every one of them.

Even his run-ins with the law were pure Cas.

When he went on trial in federal court for tax evasion, even that was a circus. This sworn testimony from his nephew, Odell Cas Lane, then a state senator, "Those checks aren't phony. Just the names on them is, that's all."

During deliberations, the jury was heard singing "The Old Rugged Cross."

Cas was acquitted. The week following the trial, at least two jurors went to work in Cas's stores.

Without notes, he held the auditorium enthralled for an hour. The jaw drops were audible.

Regarding running for mayor:

Cas said he and his people cruised Knoxville in the hours after midnight on election day looking for the down and out, the more down and out the better, the grungier the better. They then hired one for each polling place, gave them five bucks and a half-pint, and gave them his opponent's literature to hand out. Each was followed by a little girl, also hired for each polling place, each in pigtails, with instructions to hand out flyers for Cass with the line, "Won't you vote for my Uncle Cass?"

Regarding the specials he hawked on TV:

"Here's what you do," he told us. "Plan ahead. Inch up the price of, say, green beans a bit at a time for four weeks, then have a special on green beans at the original price. Folks will think they're saving a bunch, they'll buy all your beans, and you haven't discounted anything."

Regarding new store openings:

Send everybody in the surrounding neighborhood a bill, varying the amount owed. When they show up at the store outraged, you apologize for the mistake, and give them coupons for merchandise you've marked up to cover – see the green beans example.

"People are simple," he said, "you can herd 'em like cattle."

Regarding store security:

To quote Cas from his TV spot, "If you just look like you're up to somethin' in our store, we're gonna whoop hell outa you, and swear you jumped us. The police will just put you in jail for 10 days. We're gonna put you in the hospital for 10 days."

On promotions:

The splashier – my word – the better to make sure you draw a crowd.

Example One: Chicken Tossing Days

Take several crates of live chickens up on the roof of the store.

Take a chicken out, walk to the edge of the roof, wring its neck, and throw it out to the crowd below, if you catch it, you keep it.

Repeat. Frenzy assured.

Example Two: Dog Dipping Days

Build a circular vat/pool in the parking lot, say, a foot to two feet high, maybe 15 across, fill it with water and flea and tick solution. If you buy x amount of groceries, you can dip your dog in the pool, one dog (or other) at a time.

People will come out from all of the hills, coves, and hollers, bring all their dogs, and buy all your groceries, Cas assured us, and that's not all.

People would walk their mules and horses in there, get in with them, and splash the toxic stew all over them.

Best part, people would put their kids in there for a once-over rinse.

Example Three: Bury someone alive in your parking lot

Digger O'Dell had a schtick of burying himself alive and surviving. He breathed through a tube and evidently got soup through it, too. Cas buried Digger in a glass coffin with a camera in the parking lot of his Chapman Highway store. Buy x amount if groceries and you could take a look at Digger down there.

The deal was for 30 days, but Digger started to suffer from severe claustrophobia well short of that, and begged to be brought up. Deal's a deal, said Cas, and made him stay down there the whole 30 days

Then there were other stories, like the one about cops and prostitutes – about running all the pimps out of town while mayor, and then letting the cops pimp the prostitutes – much safer and more efficient.

Listening to Cas that day was for the audience much like the people watching Digger suffer down there. You aren't proud of it, but you couldn't look away.

Bill Haltom tells a story about Cas.

When Bill was in law school in the mid to late 70s, the Butcher brothers, Jake and C.H., were pushing the Knoxville World's Fair. Cas divided everybody into two categories, Hill People and Valley People. He and his were Hill People. He said Valley People would make a ton of money off the World's Fair, and Hill People would pay for it.

He was nothing if not insightful.

I think about Cas even today, especially today. Rough around the edges, in fact, all the way to his very center, we dismiss him at our own risk.

Change that bad blue suit to a good blue suit, dye that wispy white hair blond and comb it over, change Knoxville to New York.

NEVER OVER THE HILL

All we're talking about is scale.

Cas's kind of amoral populism elected a President in 2016.

You got to ask yourself: Are you waiting for a chicken, or are you the chicken?

– Dan Conaway

"IT'S FOOTBALL TIME IN TENNESSEE!"

And other games and game-changing moments in all the shades of orange. "That, Bill Anderson, is the way you do it. Give. Him. Six."

"And then, in the late in the third quarter with the Vols trailing 17-10, he made the greatest comeback since Lazarus."

"GIVE HIM SIX" – GREAT MEMORIES OF UT FOOTBALL IN THE SIXTIES AND SEVENTIES

The legendary Voice of the Vols, John Ward, had many great phrases. One of his best was his proclamation anytime a Vol scored a touchdown: "Give him six!"

Dan and I have made our own Give Him Six list. Our top six memories of UT football during our years on The Hill.

Number Six:

The day John Ward first announced, "It's football time in Tennessee!" September 14, 1968.

Read about it in Dan's chapter on the Tennessee-Georgia game on Doug's rug.

Number Five:

The Crossville Comet takes off into the end zone and then flies off as a Blue Angel. December 20, 1971, The Liberty Bowl.

John Ward called Vol fullback Curt Watson, who hailed from Crossville, Tennessee, the "Crossville Comet." In the closing minutes of the first ever meeting of Tennessee and Arkansas, the Comet soared into the end zone for the winning touchdown.

And he didn't stop there.

NEVER OVER THE HILL

After graduation he joined the U.S. Navy and became a part of its legendary flight squadron, the Blue Angels. In his extraordinary career as a Navy Pilot, in 1985, he took Tom Cruise on a flight to prepare him for his role in the original film version of "Top Gun."

Number Four:

The Vols welcome Doug Dickey back to Knoxville. October 24, 1970.

Vols head football coach Doug Dickey had left UT at the end of the 1969 season to return to his Alma Mater, the University of Florida.

He brought his Gators to Knoxville in 1970 to play the Volunteers then coached by his successor, 28-year-old Bill Battle, who was barely older than many of his players.

Battle's Vols blew out the Gators, 38-7. Coach Dickey regretted leaving Knoxville as evidenced by the fact that he returned to UT in 1985 to be UT Athletic Director.

Number Three:

Johnny comes marching home, and Bill Battle bids a classic farewell, 1976.

In 1976, UT fired Coach Battle and brought back to The Hill the legendary Vol, Johnny Majors, who had just won a national championship at Pittsburgh. In his final "Bill Battle TV Show", the fired coach said goodbye, remembering, "My father taught me years ago that when they are running you out of town, make it look like you are leading a parade!"

Number Two:

Rocky Top arrives at Neyland Stadium, October 21, 1972.

At halftime of the Tennessee-Alabama game, the Pride of the Southland played for the first time a song written by Felice and Boudleaux Bryant in 1967, and first recorded by the Osbourne Brothers that same year.

Pride conductor Dr. WJ Julian was at first reluctant for the band to play it. But with the encouragement of band members, the Pride played it at halftime during the third Saturday in October. The song was "Rocky Top", and Vol fans have been singing it while the Pride has played it ever since.

And the Number One greatest memory of Vol football during our years on The Hill…

Condredge's Comeback. September 7, 1974.

Condredge Holloway arrived on The Hill in 1971, destined to be the first African American quarterback in the Southeastern Conference. In the first game of the 1974 season, he in effect made the greatest comeback in the history of Tennessee football.

And it was literally a comeback.

Early in the season opening game against UCLA, he appeared to have suffered a serious injury and had to be carried off the field and transported to UT Hospital, where he was treated for an apparent shoulder separation.

And then, late in the third quarter with the Vols trailing 17-10, he made the greatest comeback since Lazarus.

He appeared from the Vols' dressing room on the east side of the stadium, raced across the back of the north end zone, and then the west sideline to the Vols bench, as the crowd went berserk.

He told Coach Bill Battle he was ready to go back in the game. He promptly led the Vols down Shields-Watkins Field on a drive that culminated

NEVER OVER THE HILL

with a 12-yard touchdown run by Holloway as he hurdled three UCLA defenders at the goal line, landing on his head in the end zone.

Holloway had to be helped off the field again after his courageous leaping run, and barefoot place kicker Ricky Townsend kicked the extra point that gave the Vols a 17-17 tie that felt like a win.

It was a comeback we will never forget.

– Bill Haltom

"I didn't know if that made the news or if that student was caught and eaten whole by Rin Tin Tin, but I decided since student was the flavor of the night, I wasn't going to hang around to be served."

JUST ANOTHER SATURDAY: RANKINGS, PANTY RAIDS, GERMAN SHEPHERDS, AND DORM CLIMBING

By mid-November of 1967, Tennessee was on a six-game winning streak. Despite a season-opening loss to UCLA in Los Angeles, the Vols were now ranked number two in the country, and UCLA was ranked number one.

When Saturday, November 18 dawned, we were set to play Ole Miss in Jackson, Mississippi.

When I put my head down that night – actually, very early the next morning – I had pushed through crowds, evaded campus cops, city cops, and dogs, scaled walls, and squeezed through my dorm room window to make it to my bed.

We beat Ole Miss that day to go 7-and-1. Later, UCLA would lose to go 7-1-and-1. We – just about all 26,000 of us – did the math. Number two had won. Number one had lost.

Ergo ...

WE WERE NUMBER ONE!

That's what we were screaming when we emptied every dorm, every apartment, every fraternity house – everywhere – and filled the campus, and the Cumberland Strip with students ready for a party.

And we had one.

Big enough to bring traffic to a halt, to bring everything but the celebration to a halt. Commerce on Cumberland was choked off as students filled the street, climbed over stopped cars, and got completely out of control. Stores were swamped. Things were taken. Things were broken. Windows were broken. Noses were broken as fights broke out. Order was broken.

And the police – campus cops and city cops – all the police – were called and came.

Meanwhile, I found myself with a few thousand of my best friends in front of West A, a women's dorm with an unimaginative name, like the women's dorm next to it, West B.

West A was having a full-fledged panty raid of epic proportion, the eponymous article of clothing flying out of countless open windows to the cheering crowd below. As if that wasn't entertaining enough, there was another show going on starring a naked male student and the campus police chasing him.

He was streaking. I didn't know that was a thing. College is about discovery.

What made it particularly interesting was the fact that this guy was *inside* West A and so were the cops. He would make an occasional appearance in a second-floor window, announced by the screams of the girls in that window's room, and then take off again, mere steps ahead of UT's finest in pursuit.

West A had an entrance structure, an addition of mostly glass tacked onto the front to protect people coming in and out and block the lobby from weather. The flat roof of that lined up with the windowsills of five or six of the rooms on the second floor.

Our guy climbed through a window at one end and raced across the roof, leaping full-speed into a tree at the far end – into a holly tree – naked – all those prickly leaves, all the way down.

NEVER OVER THE HILL

He emerged at the bottom, bloody but unbowed, arms raised as he raced around the side and disappeared into the dark, cops watching from above.

The applause was thunderous.

From there, I pressed myself into the mass of bodies on the pedestrian bridge over Cumberland which afforded a view east and west of the chaos below.

East toward the Hill, two police vans were inching forward with Knoxville cops in front and behind grabbing students at random and handing them off to the waiting arms of fellow cops standing in the open doors of the vans.

Ironically, this was happening right in front of the UT Law School.

West toward The Strip, two other vans were stopped with lights blazing and cameras rolling as two competing Knoxville TV stations were covering the roiling scene live for the 11 o'clock news. I eased off the bridge on the south side and headed west since the north side was about to be boarded by yet more cops.

When I crossed 17th, I saw the same thing a couple of the cameras did. Several canine patrols were in the street barely holding back barking and snarling German Shepherds. One officer let his loose to chase a student down an alley between buildings.

I didn't know if that made the news or if that student was caught and eaten whole by Rin Tin Tin, but I decided since student was the flavor of the night, I wasn't going to hang around to be served.

The Kappa Sig house was a short block up 17th, so I ducked in there. I wasn't one of them but this night we were all one in the spirit if not all one in the dog bowl, so they took me in. The scene on The Strip was the scene on their TV in the chapter living room.

Several beers later, I ventured back out and worked my way back toward my dorm, Reese Hall in the Presidential Complex, so named because all the dorms in it were named after former UT presidents: Reese for men, Carrick South for men, Carrick North for women, and Humes for women.

They were brand-new my freshman year, the latest of everything. They tore them down recently because they were so hopelessly out-of-date.

I understand they may soon tear down what's left of me.

Anyway, as I reached the bridge from the courtyard to Reese's front door, I noticed a line of students waiting to get in. At the door, someone official was taking up their student activities cards. A guy at the back of the line told me that we would all have to report to the administration building the next day and account for our behavior in order to get them back.

One couldn't avail oneself of student benefits without that card, get food in the complex cafeteria, do business at the drop-and-add window (more about that elsewhere), get tickets to student concerts or events, get grades at the end of the quarter …

One couldn't get football tickets without that card, people.

Nope. I wasn't giving up that card.

I backed out of the line and wandered beneath the bridge to the ground floor. After locating my second-floor window, I studied the wall beneath it. It had decorative concrete ridges about every fourth row of bricks.

This was doable.

I threw pebbles at the window to see if my roommate Pete Bale was in there. Nothing. I tried the hoarse stage whisper, "Bale." No response. Finally, I screamed, "BALE!" He came to the window. If the guys on the bridge heard me, they could care less.

NEVER OVER THE HILL

With gestures and another stage whisper, I told Pete I was coming up. I did, scaling the wall like a drunk Spiderman. The window was the flip-open kind, leaving an opening of maybe 10" above and below the level open pane.

I squeezed through that hole. I weighed 150 pounds in the fall of 1967. Today, I couldn't get my leg through that hole. But then, I wouldn't climb that wall either. In 1967, I didn't know I couldn't do that, so I did.

An apt description of much of my college career, my whole career actually.

The next day, we got some more news.

WE WEREN'T NUMBER ONE!

In their infinite wisdom, those who do college rankings left us at number two and moved USC all the way from number four to number one.

As far as I was concerned, that was a big pile of number two.

However, I'll always have the memory of a naked guy cutting himself to shreds in a holly tree.

Some things you just can't ever un-see.

– Dan Conaway

"*Mears asked Ward to develop a brand for UT sports. Together they came up with 'Big Orange Country', and the rest, as they say, is Vol history.*"

"*And so female high school basketball players were restricted to a half-court game even though no one had ever seen a dropped uterus on a basketball court.*"

HOW RAY MEARS CHANGED THE IMAGE OF UT, AND PAT SUMMITT CHANGED THE GAME FOREVER

There were two great basketball coaches at UT in the 70s.

One wore an orange blazer and changed the image of the university. The other changed the game of basketball forever, by executing a full court press in a courtroom that opened scholarships and sports to the women of America.

Ray Mears arrived at UT in 1962 after winning the NCAA College Division basketball national championship at Wittenberg University in Ohio.

He immediately started building a basketball program at UT that would win three SEC championships and beat Kentucky many times. But he did more than that. Donning his trademark orange blazer, he created Big Orange Country.

And he did that by teaming up with a young advertising agent who would become the voice of Tennessee sports.

Ray Mears was more than a basketball coach. He was a promoter, the sports equivalent of P.T. Barnum. He not only recruited great basketball players to UT, notably Ernie Grunfeld and Bernard King. He also recruited John Ward whose voice made Tennessee basketball and football come alive for radio listeners across the Volunteer State.

John Ward graduated from UT Law School, but never practiced law. He practiced advertising. In 1962, the new UT basketball coach delivered Ward a new client, the University of Tennessee athletics program.

Coach Mears asked Ward to develop a brand for UT sports. Together they came up with "Big Orange Country", and the rest, as they say, is Vol history.

In 1965, Ward became the voice of Tennessee basketball on the Vol Radio Network, and in 1967 became the voice for Tennessee football as well, proclaiming, "It's football time in Tennessee!"

Coach Mears kept promoting the Big Orange brand not only by winning basketball games, but by putting on a show at Stokely Athletic Center. In the Vols' pre-game warmups, Mears had the pep band play "Sweet Georgia Brown" while the team performed a pre-game show featuring a player on an orange unicycle who juggled 3 basketballs and then drove the unicycle to the basketball goal for what was literally a lay-up. The crowd went wild!

The unicyclist was Roger Peltz. He had played high school basketball at Rockwood High School in Roane County. Standing on a basketball court, he could hardly make a free throw. But on one wheel, he was fantastic.

He walked on, or rather rode on, to the Vol basketball team when Coach Mears saw his unique talent as a juggling unicyclist. Roger later became a stand-up comedian in Las Vegas and a voice on Hanna Barbera cartoons.

And while neither could ride unicycles, Ernie Grunfeld and Bernard King were found in New York City by Coach Mears and Assistant Coach Stu Aberdeen. They were brought to Knoxville where they delivered the most exciting basketball in Tennessee history.

In the fall of 1974, another basketball coach arrived at UT. Pat Head, later to become Pat Head Summitt, became the Lady Vols basketball coach at the age of 21, after being an All-American at UT Martin.

There weren't many Lady Vols fans at UT in 1974, as they weren't many womens' college basketball fans anywhere. At her first game as Lady Vols coach in December of 1974, it was not standing room only at Alumni Gym.

There were 52 fans in attendance.

NEVER OVER THE HILL

Pat later recalled, "We had an announcer on the PA system to introduce the starting lineups. But it occurred to me that maybe we should just have everyone in attendance stand and introduce themselves!"

But over the next 38 years, Coach Summitt's Lady Vols played before more than 52 fans. They played before sell-out crowds at UT and in arenas across the country as millions watched the games on ESPN and other networks.

She literally created NCAA women's basketball that did not even exist in 1974.

She won eight national championships and 1,098 games. But she did something even more phenomenal. She changed the game of basketball forever, and she did it not only on a basketball court, but in a courtroom.

When Pat Head became the Lady Vols coach in 1974, girls playing high school basketball in Tennessee and in many high schools across America, were not allowed to play full court basketball.

Incredibly, the prevailing wisdom (SIC) at the time was that it was dangerous for girls to run full court, as it could damage their reproductive systems. So-called physical education experts said that running the length of a basketball court could cause a young woman's uterus to fall out.

Seriously.

And so female high school basketball players were restricted to a half-court game even though no one had ever seen a dropped uterus on a basketball court.

Pat Head herself had not been allowed to play full court basketball at Ashland City High School in west Tennessee. She thought this was ridiculous, and in her early years as Lady Vols coach she changed the game with literally a full-court press.

In 1976, Victoria Cape, a high school basketball player in Oak Ridge, Tennessee, filed a lawsuit against the Tennessee Secondary School Athletic

Association (TSSAA), claiming the rules restricting high school female basketball players to a half-court game violated Title IX, a law passed by Congress in 1972 that read, "No person in the United States shall, on the basis of sex, be excluded from participation in, be denied the benefits of, or be subject to discrimination under any education program or activity receiving any Federal financial assistance."

Coach Pat joined the legal team for Victoria Cape in this case, serving as an expert witness. In her testimony at the trial in the United States Federal Court for the Eastern District of Tennessee, she prophesied the future of women's basketball.

She told the Court that because of Title IX, there would soon be an NCAA Women's basketball division, and that women would get athletic scholarships to college.

She accurately forecast that it would open doors to the young women of America, not only at basketball arenas, but to colleges and much more. She further testified that if Victoria Cape and high school female basketball players in Tennessee were not allowed to play full court basketball, they would not receive athletic scholarships to play college basketball as the women's college game had expanded to full court.

Coach Pat's expert testimony led to a verdict for Victoria Cape and a ruling opening the full court to female players. A protracted legal battle followed, but in 1978, Coach Pat prevailed in getting the TSSAA to drop the half-court game and let female basketball players run the court.

Coach Pat Summitt went on to win more than national championships. In her 38 years as Lady Vols' coach, she graduated 100 percent of her players, and changed the game of basketball forever.

– Bill Haltom

"He let the pass go and McClain pulled it in at the Georgia 48. First and ten, Tennessee. First ever, SEC."

MOVING THE CHAINS

Georgia scored again while I was throwing up.

Georgia and I had already done these things several times in the preceding three hours, but, like Tennessee, I didn't think I had anything left to counter this time. Late, very late, in the fourth quarter, our offense had gone ice cold and we were down by eight – and my temperature was red hot, up by two. The governor, the first Senator Gore, a gaggle of congressmen … even the head tire kicker at Goodyear whose blimp hovered above … were watching from various swell box seats. Millions were watching on TV and even ABC's saccharine Chris Schenkel (this guy makes Jim Nance sound like the grim reaper) thought Uga had this one all wrapped up.

I was watching from the couch in the ATO house tube room, alternating between teeth-rattling chills and wind sprints to the john, all wrapped up in a blanket.

It was the first and only home game I would miss in my four years at UT. It was the first and only home game UT wouldn't win during those four magic years. It was our first game played on artificial turf – dubbed Doug's Rug for Coach Dickey. It was the very first game and the very first catch for #85 in your Tennessee program, a shy sophomore from Nashville named Lester McClain.

It was a remarkable game.

Bubba Wyche (is that a good quarterback name, or what?) was staring at fourth down. Fans poured from Neyland, resigned to loss, and the clock ran faster than any of our backs had all day. He let the pass go and McClain pulled it in at the Georgia 48.

First and ten, Tennessee. First ever, SEC.

That pass gave us a chance, gave us hope. It changed the game, and the way the game is played. Lester McLain is Black. Two Black players had gone before him at Kentucky, but neither had lettered since you couldn't play varsity as a freshman, and their careers were ended by injury and heartbreak. Lester's roommate his freshman year, also Black, didn't come back his sophomore year. So, with that catch, Lester McClain broke through the varsity football color line in the SEC and moved the chains.

It was an amazing game.

Later in the drive and facing another fourth down, Bubba moved the Vols to the line quickly and fired a touchdown pass to Gary Kreis as the clock rolled up all zeros – and I knocked over a pitcher and fell off the couch. Bubba then hit Ken DeLong for the two-point conversion and Tennessee tied Georgia – as Chris and me, and those loyal, hopeful fans still in the stadium, all went insane. I charged to the front porch, blanket flapping and heaves forgotten, and screamed at the throngs headed to their cars, completely unaware of the final result, and staring unbelievably at the leaping, ragged frat boy specter before them bearing the improbable news in boxers and blanket.

It was a miraculous game.

From the east upper deck, student seats in my day, the world looks promising. On one side, sheer cliffs rise from a river dotted with boats in a moored parade and distant blue-green mountains form the backdrop. On the other, the buildings that house the means to be any and everything stand watch over dreams on a hill. Below, a contest unfolds that is no more serious than a game but every bit as serious as things that have gone before and are yet to come.

For more people than any other sport, I think, the beginning of football season is about hope and renewal, a slate wiped clean for whatever's next, shared in mass mutual anticipation on a huge stage or by just one sick kid on a couch.

1968 was the symbolic year of the tragedy of Martin Luther King in the spring, of Bobby Kennedy in the summer, and of the hope symbolized in one young man catching a ball in the fall.

When Lester McClain caught that fourth down pass, he wasn't Black or white. He was orange. And he was red, white, and blue.

– Dan Conaway

"But we Volunteers were the first to phrase the great question, thanks to a Florida State University graduate named Burt Reynolds."

HOW 'BOUT THAT BURT?

College students and alumni across America have unique greetings for their fellow and sister classmates and alumni.

University of Virginia students and alumni shout "Wahoowa" to one another. Ole Miss folks yell "Hoddy Toddy!" Arkansas calls the hogs, "Woo, pig! Sooee!" And University of Georgia grads inexplicably just bark at each other.

But we Volunteers have our own unique greeting that is actually a rhetorical question: "HOW 'BOUT THEM VOLS?!!!!"

Fans, students, and alumni of other lesser institutions of higher education have plagiarized the line, as you will occasionally hear Kentucky fans chant "How 'bout them Cats?," or Vandy students pathetically ask, "Would you please tell me the current condition of those Commodores?"

But we Volunteers were the first to phrase the great question, thanks to a Florida State University graduate named Burt Reynolds.

In a memorable scene from his 1975 flick "W.W. and Dixie Dance Kings", Reynold pulls into a service station somewhere deep in the heart of Dixie to fill up his Oldsmobile Rocket 88.

He tries to strike up a conversation with the crochety old station attendant, asking him, "How 'bout them Tennessee Vols? They gonna go all the way this year, aren't they?"

The gas station attendant, who was apparently a Bama fan, gruffly responds, "I don't give no dog about no Tennessee Vols."

We orange-blooded folks who do give a dog (Smokey) about our Vols soon embraced the line and shared or yelled it to one another after a Vol win. To this day, nearly 50 years after Burt uttered it, we Vols still ask that orange rhetorical question to one another.

Another great Vol chant is…."IT'S GREAT…TO BE…A TEN-NES-SEE VOL!" Thousands of us chant it in unison as we leave Neyland Stadium after a big win.

Dan, my co-author favors, "T - E - DOUBLE N - E - DOUBLE S - DOUBLE E - TENNESSEE!"

He feels spelling has never been a strong suit for us and requires reinforcement.

Again, students and fans at other schools have tried to steal the line. But "It's great…to be…a Flor-i-da Ga-Ter" just doesn't roll of the tongue, lacking the rhythm, meter, and near iambic pentameter of Tennessee's proud line.

And, frankly, it's not great to be a swamp-dwelling reptile that eats whoever and whatever happens to be at the edge of a Florida backyard at any given moment. Pets, family members, picnic tables, small sports cars.

And then there is one single word yelled by us Volunteers during the middle of a classic Tennessee song. The word is "Woo!" (no "pig sooee"). Thousands of us sing it, albeit off key. when the Pride of the Southland plays "Rocky Top!"

No, we didn't steal the "Woo" from the Razorbacks. We're calling a dog. They're calling a pig. You choose which one you want to come jump in your lap in the living room.

So, here's to you, old Tennessee! "T - E - Double N - E - Double S - Double E - Tennessee!"

How 'bout them Vols?

The answer is "It's great…to be…a Ten-nes-see Vol!… WOO!!!!"

– *Bill Haltom*

"The drum major was pledge Satch Sanders. He had a tall piece of rolled cardboard for a hat, some sort of Carnicus costume coat, rubber boots, and a bathroom plunger for a baton."

PRIDE OF THE FRATLAND BAND AND ICE DIVING

My sophomore year, we had a pretty good interfraternity council intramural flag football team – frat league for short – and we had a pretty good record – we beat the SAEs for short.

We had a number of guys who had played high school football, and some earnest guys around them. We also had some All-American creativity.

Down the street, they were playing big-boy football in Neyland Stadium. In my four years, we never lost a home game and beat Alabama four straight times.

We also had the Pride of the Southland Band.

Most colleges don't even remember the band, or if they even had one. When most bands started to play, fans went to the head, or the concessions, or to meet somebody during halftime, or they glued a transistor radio to the side of their heads to get the scores and updates, or the game stats so far ... or all of the above.

Vols fans come to the stadium early to listen to the band and watch their intricate pre-game routines. That includes the drum major running out – in an impossibly tall hat, kicking his legs impossibly high, and leaning back at an impossible angle – to lead the band in forming the T the team will run through entering the field, during which I'm pretty sure there are a number of people who pass out screaming, and heart attacks are fairly common.

At halftime, Vol fans watch their band's performance eat the lunch of the opposing team's band and the bus they came in. We have – and you can check me on this – never lost a halftime.

That included a kind of trademark for the Pride of the Southland Band – something called a circle drill – that has drawn the praise of every network TV announcer that's seen it from UT's own Lindsey Nelson to Keith Jackson in my day, to Jim Nance, to whoever's up there.

Obviously, the band forms a circle, and then a circle within a circle and so on, and then those circles alternate in opposite directions, clockwise and counterclockwise, until the stadium thinks it's watching a kaleidoscope down there.

Meanwhile, one weekday afternoon, ATO is playing somebody on the athletic field across the street from frat row.

Before the game starts, everybody is gathered on the sidelines for – uh – refreshments. Let's just say, it wasn't Gatorade.

Before the game starts, there's an announcement through the loudspeaker. There wasn't a loudspeaker. There was now. Somebody had put together extension cords from a light pole plug to a portable speaker, drug all of that to midfield, and was talking into a crackling microphone:

"LADIES AND GENTLEMEN ... YOUR ATTENTION PLEASE," said one of our pledges, or maybe an active, I just can't remember nor can any of my ancient brothers, "PLEASE WELCOME THE PRIDE OF THE FRATLAND BAND!"

And out they marched.

The drum major was pledge Satch Sanders. He had a tall piece of rolled cardboard for a hat, some sort of Carnicus (campus theatrical, more about that later) costume coat, rubber boots, and a bathroom plunger for a baton.

He even tried the kicks, fell down a couple of times, and got right back up and back into it. Meanwhile, both sidelines were rolling on the ground and howling.

Behind Satch, was the band, playing Tennessee's fight song, "Down The Field," very badly. On kazoos. ("Rocky Top" wasn't adopted until my co-author Bill's time).

Pledges Reggie Martin, Randy Tickle, Bill Martin, Richard – Jelly – Donner, and active Rem Owen, and a few more, whose names the ancient council couldn't come up with. Bill Martin was the drum section. The drum was a long cardboard box with slits cut in it, hung around Bill's neck with string. The drumsticks were large kitchen spoons.

Everybody was in some sort of mismatched Carnicus costume found somewhere deep in a frat house closet.

They formed up at midfield and played the National Anthem

The sidelines loved it. Order had to be restored to start the game.

And then, of course, halftime. Out they came, again playing "Down The Field." They did a circle drill, running into each other, dropping their kazoos. Then, they did something special just for our opponents.
When we played AGR, the Ag fraternity (more about them later), the band formed a hoe, and played "Farmer In The Dell" on their kazoos.

When we played the SAEs, they formed a dollar sign and played, "Money Can't Buy You Love."

And so on.

Both sidelines were laughing so hard, they couldn't breathe. Our opponents couldn't breathe.

And so on. Every game.

I was extremely pleased when Bill told me that the Pride of the Fratland Band survived into the 70s.

I think "Rocky Top" on a kazoo might just work.

All of it was Satch's idea. Satch Sanders, All-American ATO.

On to the spring games, called springfest or some such, with various intramural contests, between fraternities, between sororities, between dorms, between chemistry professors for all I know, because I was concentrating on the tug of war.

ATO had a team and I had volunteered my freshman year. Obviously and surprisingly; size and strength weren't prerequisites. Neither was taking it seriously.

I can't remember – a recurring theme – the whole team. Bob Alley was on it, maybe Kenny Clayton, and one junior – the very gung-ho Phil Critchfield – Beast. Beast was experienced. He'd lost the tug of war several times.

I forget how many to a team, but I think maybe six. Three or four pretty big, pretty strong guys ... and two or three more of us. We met a few times, pulled on a rope, talked strategy. The big guys thought they could anchor the front and back, with us creating slack in the middle, and then pull the opposing side over the line with a mighty jerk. I didn't say it was a good strategy.

We were just going to show up, give it our best, and have fun.

Meanwhile, down the row from us was the Alpha Gamma Rho house. Mostly Ag majors. We called them Alpha Grabba Hoe. Big, muscle-bound, hog-wrestling, cornfed farm boys. At least that's what they looked like out in front of their house when I passed by that spring.

Out front in full sweats in the heat. Out front with their wrists and hands wrapped in tape. Out front with two teams and a huge rope stretched tight between them, talcum powder popping off the rope in the sunlight. Out front calling cadence as they pulled, like Vikings rowing a warship across a calm sea.

NEVER OVER THE HILL

I didn't know that Alpha Grabba Hoe – forgive me, Alpha Gamma Rho, don't hurt me – lived for the spring tug of war. I didn't know that they hadn't lost a spring tug of war since there was a spring tug of war.

God help me, I didn't know.

At least I then knew why so few volunteered for the tug of war, and why we were mostly freshmen.

Then, we found out who we were pulling against in the first round.

Alpha Grabba Hoe – now Alpha Grab An ATO. The Vikings were close to shore.

We needed another strategy.

The venue for this event was impressive. In an open field right above and just east of the brand-new Tom Black Track, between the brand-new Fraternity Row and the brand-new Presidential dorm complex – lots of brand-new in those days – the university brought in a bulldozer and dug a hole for the tug of war.

It was about 12 feet long, six wide, and six deep. The eventful day, literally, it was filled with ice. The opposing teams would face each other at either end of that trench, a big, thick, white rope between them, floating in the melting ice.

When the tug began, the first person on either team pulled into the pit signaled victory for the opposing team. And all the members of the losing team were then required to jump in the icy, muddy mess.

A referee, or judge, or executioner ... your choice ... standing on the edge between the teams lifted his arms like a touchdown signal, and the two teams slowly raised the rope and pulled it taut. When he dropped his arms, it was on.

Our new strategy was pragmatic. We were going to lose – so – how do we make the most of that?

When we faced off, Beast was first on the rope. When the arms dropped, Beast pulled back with a mighty grunt, and we strained and leaned in, giving it everything we had.

And Beast went into the ice in 2.3 seconds, and I'm rounding up.

Two of our Little Sisters appeared carrying a card table and two folding chairs. Without saying a word but looking official, they set it up along one side of the pit, a bit back from the edge.

As each of us entered the pit, the Little Sisters held up cards grading our efforts from 1 to 10.

The onlookers loved it, and shouted out their own grades:

"Seven, seven, seven," they screamed, for my back flip, echoing the Little Sisters grade, although I was robbed. There was an eight, another seven, a five for a cannonball that soaked the judges, and a final ten for Beast's attempted one-and-a-half that ended in a spectacular belly flop.

The ten was for the effort, symbolic of the day.

I'm not sure anybody remembered who actually won. They definitely remembered who lost.

A winning strategy.

– Dan Conaway

"He then added that if he ran, his campaign slogan would be, 'Vote for Vince. He has something the other candidates don't have.'"

LONG LIVE QUEEN VINCE!

In October, 1970, graduate student Vince Staten was elected UT Homecoming Queen. But he never got to wear the crown. He wore a paper bag over his head instead.

Vince was a humor columnist for the Daily Beacon. His hilarious columns, "Staten's Statics," were enormously popular across the campus.

Early in the Fall Quarter of 1970, he began one of his columns with a disclaimer: "The rumors that I am running for homecoming Queen are not true." He then added that if he ran, his campaign slogan would be, "Vote for Vince. He has something the other candidates don't have."

Vince had no intention of actually running for Homecoming Queen, but students began circulating a petition for his candidacy. And he kept the jokes going and the laughs coming in his Beacon columns promoting his non-campaign as the "bra-less candidate."

He promised his supporters that if he was elected Homecoming Queen, they could join him on Shields-Watkins Field at halftime of the Homecoming game wearing paper bags on their heads. The paper bag headgear was Vince's trademark as his picture beside his Beacon column showed him so attired. He explained that he posed that way because he believed in the old joke that that was the best way to dress for a blind date.

His supporters presented the Homecoming Board with a candidacy qualifying petition signed by hundreds of students. The Homecoming Board rejected his petition on the basis that since Vince was a graduate student, he was not qualified to be Homecoming Queen. Undeterred, Vince supporters launched a write-in campaign.

NEVER OVER THE HILL

Vince urged his readers to not vote for him, saying he was the Apathy candidate.

And then the election was held, the votes were counted, and Vince was elected Homecoming Queen in a landslide. He received over 2,500 handwritten votes, 60 percent of the votes cast.

The Homecoming Board refused to certify his election. Even Queen-Elect Vince agreed that he should not be crowned, acknowledging that his candidacy was a joke.

Vince did not appear in Neyland Stadium for the Homecoming game. He spent the day hiking in the mountains. The Vols beat Kentucky that day. 45-3, on their way to an 11-1 season and a trip to the Sugar Bowl.

Vince was relieved when he heard the Vols had won. "Had the Vols lost that game to Kentucky," he recalls, "I think I know who would have been blamed!"

Non-Queen Vince went on to become a popular humor columnist for newspapers across the country. He wrote 15 very funny books, and was even a popular guest on David Letterman's Late Night TV show.

When he appeared on the Letterman show, he didn't wear a paper bag over his head.

– Bill Haltom

"The question isn't why he decided to set sail; the question is why it took him or anybody else that long. Hadn't they noticed there was a river down there?"

THE VOL NAVY: AN ORANGE CRUISE

In 1962, the then Voice of the Vols, Vol Football Network Broadcaster George Mooney, found a quicker and more enjoyable way to get from his home in west Knoxville to Neyland Stadium on football Saturdays other than fighting traffic.

He boarded his little runabout, fired up its outboard engine, and sailed the Tennessee River to the shore by the stadium.

There were no docks there at the time, so Captain Mooney tied his boat to a tree and then climbed up the rocky top shore to make his way to the press box to call the games on what was then known as the Tennessee Texaco Network.

The question isn't why he decided to set sail; the question is why it took him or anybody else that long. Hadn't they noticed there was a river down there?

Word quickly got around on how Mooney had navigated the waters of the Tennessee River to get to the stadium, and other Vol fans were soon climbing in their own watercraft to join him on a Big Orange cruise.

George Mooney's little runabout became the flagship of an orange fleet that would soon be christened "The Vol Navy" growing from one boat to hundreds.

The fleet was not just small motorboats. There were fishing boats, ski boats, canoes, kayaks, paddle boats, and even yachts up to 100 feet long.

The crews in the Vol Navy had a rollicking good time on their voyages to Neyland, decked in orange and white and blaring Vol songs from onboard PA systems. It became a massive floating tailgate party!

And almost one massive boat, since people travelled by walking and/or leaping from one boat to the next, to the next, like giant floating stepping stones. The people doing this were often floating a bit themselves.

The City of Knoxville built 600 feet of boat docks so that George Mooney and his hundreds of fellow Vol sailors would not have to moor their vessels to trees and climb to the entrance to Neyland.

It wasn't enough.

As the Vol flotilla grew, the City expanded the docks and built a pedestrian tunnel under Neyland Drive so the orange sailors could avoid Knoxville traffic even after their fleet arrived shoreside.

The Vol Navy became famous around the world as it was featured during national telecasts of Tennessee football games, particularly ESPN's College Game Day.

During my years at UT, I did not own or have access to a boat. But I managed to enlist in the Vol Navy on few wonderful football Saturdays either as a stowaway or upon invitation from a friend or, on one memorable occasion, a faculty member, to join on board their boat.

There is simply no better way to travel to Neyland Stadium for a football game than as a member of the Vol Navy.

– Bill Haltom

Smokey

UT, THE MUSICAL

The best in entertainment and enlightenment,
and some of the worst.

Getting college students to show up, pay attention,
stand in a straight line, sing – in tune,
please – dance – in step, please –
and do all of that over and over.

Hey, you try it sometime.

"At the end of the concert, the Divine Miss M passed out on the stage."

THE SHOW MUST GO ON. AND, MY FRIENDS, IT DID AND IT DOES

There's no business like show business, and during my years at UT, business was incredible.

Among the performers I saw in concert at Stokely Athletic Center were Elton John, Bette Midler, John Denver, The Beach Boys, Linda Ronstadt, Jimmy Buffett, and even the King, Elvis Presley.

The most memorable of these performances was the 1973 Homecoming Concert by Bette Midler.

At the end of the concert, the Divine Miss M passed out on the stage.

The packed house all thought it was all part of the act, and so we cheered wildly, waiting for her to stand up and do an encore.

We even cheered when aides came and carried her offstage. She did not return. We later learned that she had been transported to the UT Medical Center for care and treatment.

The Elvis concert had a similar ending.

Although the King did not collapse on the stage, when he left the building, he was carried by his assistants, the Memphis Mafia, to a waiting limousine that sped him to the McGee Tyson Airport for a quick flight back to Graceland.

In addition to the concerts, there were plays at the Clarence Brown Theater and in the round at the Carousel. I particularly remember productions of Thomas Wolf's "Look Homeward Angel" and the fabulous musical "Man of La Mancha."

I even performed one night at the Carousel, although it was not in a play.

It was in a debate! The Oxford University debate team was touring the United States and came to UT where Mark Olive and I, as members of the UT debate team, squared off against them in the round at the Carousel on the topic "Resolved: That the American Revolution was a failure!"

And then there were the annual productions of Carnicus and All Sing.

The winning 1969 Carnicus show, "Hair", was directed by none other than Dan Conaway.

All Sing was the forerunner of "Glee" and proved that sorority girls could sing. The frat boys? Well, they tried.

No list of UT performances could be complete without the marching concerts at Neyland Stadium by the Pride of the Southland Band.

Under the direction of legendary Dr W J Julian, the Pride's pregame show featured the dramatic entrance of the Volunteers running through the T.

The halftime show included the Circle Drill and other maneuvers, and the playing of the Alma Mater. And the postgame concert always included The Tennessee Waltz.

I will never forget what the Pride did during the 1972 Alabama game. For the first time, they played a song written by Felice and Boudreaux and recorded by the Osbourne Brothers in 1967.

It was "Rocky Top."

The Vols lost to Bama that day, 17-0, but the song became a part of UT music legend, remains so this day, and always will.

And of course, the Pride plays the unofficial Vol fight song, "Rocky Top," and a hundred thousand Vol fans add scream "WOO!"

– *Bill Haltom*

"'Could somebody do me?' she asked tinged with panic. 'I'd be happy to do you, my dear,' my father answered, and then did."

CALIFORNIA DREAMING AND THE AGE OF AQUARIUS

"You're in All Sing," my big brother said, "second bass."

I didn't know what All Sing was, but I knew all about second base. That was the position I played at my school, White Station Jr. High, the few times I left the bench. What singing has to do with fielding ground balls or hitting curve balls, or failing to do either of those things, was beyond me, but much of college seemed to be beyond me those first few weeks.

The analogy worked because I was seeing a lot of curve balls.

A big brother was the active (fraternity member) who volunteered to help you survive pledging and serve as a guide through the freshman maze. Some big brothers are better than others.

Ronnie Richards was the best.

He took me under his wing, and his wing was considerable. In his hometown of Brownsville, Tennessee, he was the organist of choice for his church when he was home. And the Episcopal Church. And the synagogue. And the funeral home. And anything else that had a keyboard and needed an enthusiastic set of fingers and personality.

If we still had town criers, Ronnie would have been Brownsville's, except he was the town laugher, and emcee, and master of any keyboard.

And he was the performance and musical director, choreographer and talent coach, and maestro of the ATO house. We had a grand piano because of Ronnie. And we had a pristine grand piano free of scratches, drink rings, cigarette burns, or any other marks of disrespect because of Ronnie. The rest of the furniture wasn't so lucky.

He was my big brother.

So, when he told me I was in All Sing, I was in All Sing, and awaiting further instruction.

Proposed by a student, All Sing began in 1932 as a fraternity-sorority group singing competition, and grew into a campus wide competition and event. Any group could enter with 12 to 16 members, and sing whatever they wanted as long as it passed muster with the university and the ground rules.

For instance, popular choices at the time such as Chuck Berry's My Ding-A-Ling, or anything by Doug Clark and the Hot Nuts, or any limerick set to music wouldn't make it.

We would be singing *California Dreaming* (with apologies to the Mamas & the Papas) and – to class things up – *No Man Is An Island* from the poem by John Donne set to music (with apologies to, well, everybody).

And I would be singing second bass along with two other guys who couldn't sing either. Second bass, as it turns out, is the lowest voice in a choir or singing group. We were supposed to reach down to the very depths of our souls and pull up the sound of, say, a foghorn on demand, in unison, in the right key.

All fall quarter, we practiced in the living room of the frat house around the piano in late afternoon four days a week and two hours on Sunday, driving people out at first, and attracting them later as we improved.

The competition was in winter quarter and the first round was in Alumni Gym. Somehow, we made it to the finals, also in Alumni Gym, but this time in rented tuxes on stage in front of a paying audience – a big audience.

In *California Dreaming*, the second basses blended in mostly, no isolated parts. However, in *No Man is an Island*, we got to shine.

"No man is an island" everyone sang, followed by the basses alone singing lower than a snake's belly, "No man stands alo -ooooooooooo -nnnnne," rolling out "alone" like close-by thunder.

And one of us cracked.

If you've ever heard a bass crack, or a tenor for that matter, it's fingernails across a chalk board, it's give-me-my-money-back bad. I'm not saying who cracked, and I'm not being noble. We *all* cracked. A chain reaction FUBAR.

After all, no man is an island.

Surprisingly, we didn't win, but I still sing that part in the shower, and I hit it every time. I don't know why the dogs run downstairs. Sounds good to me.

Ronnie must have seen something in me I hadn't seen, he certainly hadn't heard anything, because he asked me to co-direct Carnicus the next year with him – my sophomore year and his senior year.

Carnicus dates to 1897 when the city of Knoxville and UT held a joint event – a carnival – on UT's campus in May. Separately, UT students held an event – a circus – to help raise money for UT athletics in January.

In 1929, the carnival and the circus combined and Carnicus was born as a competitive Greek event staged by the fraternities and sororities.

Let's pause a moment here to reflect. Frats and sororities helped finance athletics? In my day, we had trouble paying the utility bill. Frats and sororities held a circus? In my day, Monday was a circus in the frat house. Every day was a circus.

By the time I showed up, Carnicus was the highlight of spring quarter.

Fraternities, sororities, dorms – any group – could compete. There were three categories: men, women, and mixed.

The skits were innovative, surprisingly complicated in their music, choreography, and stagecraft, brutal in their satirical attack on campus figures, always funny, and borderline raunchy. Okay, completely raunchy. Some were disqualified on that basis.

In 1969, we teamed up with AOPi sorority under Ronnie's and my direction. We hired two students to write the skit, Chris Whittle and Phil Moffitt. They had written Carnicus skits before as a team, and somebody recommended them to us.

We were going to do our version of *Hair*, the smash Broadway hit of 1968.

Turns out Whittle and Moffitt were pretty good. Good enough to start the 13-30 Corporation together and good enough to buy Esquire magazine in 1979. Whittle was elected student body president in 1969, and would later transform an entire city block of downtown Knoxville into an Oxford-esque headquarters for his various companies and education initiatives. Moffitt would go on to be ordained to teach Vipassana meditation and found the Life Balance Institute.

If I'd known these guys were going to become that deep and accomplished, I wouldn't have rewritten their script like I did. What did I know?

We had a blast.

We practiced in the ATO house basement, running into each other at the beginning, sounding terrible, but we got better and better. More confident. More trusting of each other.

The *Age of Aquarius* became the *Age of Hairy Us*, and so on. We did it all except the nude scene. The ATOs were up for it, but the AOPis and UT were not. The guys had to wear wigs because our hair was insufficiently long. We had tie-dyed and bell-bottomed everything.

We even opened like the Broadway show, coming down the aisles and handing out flowers to the audience.

Kenny Clayton did a solo in drag, dressed in a more than amply stuffed top, a very short skirt, and a very long red wig. Kenny's legs were carpeted in hair, and he had a beard. The combination of all that was impressive.

His dance routine brought the audience to their feet.

However, the best Carnicus line might have been my father's ad lib.

My parents came for the show, and were in the fraternity house lobby during the final mayhem before we left for Alumni Gym. We had to get into our costumes in the house, because there were no separate dressing rooms at the gym for all the competitors.

Jan Campbell was a UT cheerleader, an AOPi, and an ATO Little Sister that spring. The next year, she would become the ATO Sweetheart. This evening, she was a cast member, and she burst out of the women's bathroom holding her halter top on in the front with both hands, and the back wide open, needing somebody to tie the dangling strings.

"Could somebody do me?" she asked tinged with panic.

"I'd be happy to do you, my dear," my father answered, and then did. Everybody howled and the tension was broken. Attaboy, Dad.

We won.

All this time later, I still can't quite believe it.
We won.

And I found out I had skill sets I'd never exercised. Directing people. More, directing people to believe in themselves, to discover the creative side of themselves, and to let it come out and play.

Ronnie Richards saw that in me, and for that and more I'm forever grateful.

Thanks, big brother.

– Dan Conaway

"A number of the student stars of such shows went on to perform on Broadway, and in movies and TV."

HUNTER HILLS THEATRE: STUDENT STARS UNDER THE STARS

During the 60s and 70s, Clarence Brown Theatre and Carousel Theatre were not the only venues for UT students to take the stage for the performing arts. Just 40 miles away from the campus was a theatre under the stars in the Smoky Mountains.

Hunter Hills Theatre was an outdoor amphitheater that had been given to the university in 1966 by alumnus R.S. Maples and his wife Wilma. It had three stages, 2,600 seats, a concession area, and parking spaces for over 1,000 cars.

From 1966 until 1978, the UT Theatre Department had summer stock productions at the mountainside theatre with UT students starring in "Annie Get Your Gun," "Carousel," "Oklahoma," "Lil Abner" and countless other shows.

The most popular production each summer was "Dark of The Moon," the dramatic interpretation of the folk ballad of "Barbara Allen" set in the Smokies.

I recall sitting in the audience at Hunter Hills on a summer night watching the play while I was literally under the dark of the Moon. No theatre on Broadway or movie studio in Hollywood could match that atmosphere.

Hunter Hills productions were attended by thousands over the years, many in the audiences being tourists visiting nearby Gatlinburg.

A number of the student stars of such shows went on to perform on Broadway, and in movies and TV.

NEVER OVER THE HILL

David Keith started his acting career at Hunter Hills Theatre and went on to star in films such as "An Officer and a Gentleman," for which he was nominated for a Golden Globe.

He also appeared on the sidelines live at Neyland Stadium on autumn Saturdays over the years in effect playing the role of an assistant football coach!

Knoxville's own Dale Dickey appeared in many summer productions at Hunter Hills and then went to Broadway where she starred in revivals of "A Streetcar Named Desire" and "Sweeney Todd." She then went to Hollywood where she appeared in over 60 movies and television shows, becoming recognized as America's "consummate character actor."

There was no business-like show business at the University of Tennessee in the 60s and 70s at Clarence Brown and Carousel Theatres, and under the stars and both the light and the dark of the Moon at Hunter Hills.

– Bill Haltom

CAMPUS CAUSES AND CAUSATIONS

Going fishing at the Supreme Court, et al.

"Anybody going to the protest? I need a ride."

"I'm not sure how they tried to do that. You can't bus a fish."

FROM BILLY GRAHAM AND RICHARD NIXON TO THE KNOXVILLE 22, AND, OF COURSE, THE SNAIL DARTER

The UT student body was very conservative in the late 60s and well into the 70s. I once wrote in a column in the *Daily Beacon* that most of us students at the time were pursuing Bachelor of Conservative Arts degrees.

But there were a few occasions in that era when many students engaged in protests and supported causes.

These ranged from a religious crusade in Neyland Stadium featuring a sermon by President Richard Nixon, to the selection of a UT President, to the survival of a very small fish.

On the evening of May 28, 1970, 75,000 people packed Neyland Stadium. They didn't come there to see a football game. The Vols wouldn't kick off their 1970 season for another four months.

They didn't come to the stadium to hear a concert, although Ethel Waters would sing there that night accompanied by a huge choir from churches across East Tennessee.

College football stadiums in the south have often been compared to cathedrals. But in a very real sense Neyland Stadium was a cathedral that spring evening as thousands came to hear a preacher.

Not just any preacher, but the man known as "America's preacher," the famed evangelist Billy Graham.

It was the seventh night of a ten-day Graham crusade and was designated "Youth Night."

NEVER OVER THE HILL

Dr. Graham did preach that night, but he was not the only speaker who addressed the crowd that from the pulpit on the platform that had been built in the north end zone.

The other speaker was the 37th President of the United States, Richard M. Nixon.

President Nixon was a controversial figure on college campuses that spring due to the recent invasion of Cambodia in the expansion of the Vietnam War. Students were protesting on campuses across the country, and earlier that month four students had been shot and killed by National Guardsmen on the campus of Kent State University during such a protest.

Billy Graham was a close friend of President Nixon and an ardent supporter of the expansion of the war. Graham sought to have Nixon as a youth night speaker on the UT campus to demonstrate youth support.

But there was another demonstration that night, and not the one Dr. Graham hoped to see.

Among the thousands that gathered in the stadium that night were several hundred UT students and faculty members who had come not to worship but to protest the President and his expanded war effort in Vietnam and Cambodia.

A number of these protesters carried signs that read, "THOU SHALT NOT KILL."
Knoxville police confiscated many of the signs as the protesters entered the stadium.

Billy Graham introduced President Nixon, calling the recent invasion of Cambodia "a courageous act", and the overwhelming majority of the crowd gave him a warm and long ovation.

But many of the student and faculty protesters chanted "Peace!" while other stood in silence. The crowd booed them, and Knoxville Police took photos of them.

The evening ended with an altar call as Ethel Waters and the choir sang "Just As I Am." The protesters didn't answer that call.

They just silently left the stadium.

In the days that followed, warrants were served on 47 of the protesters, identified in the police photos. They were charged with disorderly conduct or disrupting a religious service, a rarely prosecuted misdemeanor under Tennessee law.

One of those cited was Dr. Charles Reynolds, a UT Religious Studies Professor who would later become the founding editor of the National Journal of Religious Ethics.

When President Nixon learned of the citations, he publicly asked that the protesters not be prosecuted. Billy Graham joined in this request, saying he loved the protesting students whom he believed had simply been "misled."

But the Mayor of Knoxville vowed to pursue every case.

Most of the protesters who were charged paid small fines. But Dr. Reynolds appealed his conviction all the way to the United States Supreme Court, claiming that his silent protest that night at Neyland Stadium had been an exercise of his First Amendment rights. The Supreme Court declined to hear his case.

A few months earlier, several hundred students had marched up The Hill and blocked the doors to the administration building after the Board of Trustees had announced the selection of Dr. Edward Boling as President of the university following the retirement of Dr. Andy Holt.

NEVER OVER THE HILL

The protesting students objected to what they claimed was lack of student or faculty consideration in the process.

When the protesting students refused to disperse, Knoxville and campus police arrived to break up the protest. It did not go well, and in the resulting scuffle (called a riot by the Knoxville media), four police and seven protesters were injured, and 22 people were arrested and charged with inciting riots.

They became known as "the Knoxville 22." The incident had UT students and faculty and the Knoxville community either denouncing or supporting the University administration for its handling of the protest.

My co-author was present for that protest, but spent most of it in a thorn bush. His account follows.

A far more peaceful protest or cause emerged on the campus a few years later, and this one, believe it or not, involved a fish. It was a tiny little fish that was only three and a half inches long and lived in the freshwaters of river and creeks in East Tennessee.

The fish was the snail darter, and it became a cause celeb on campus, particularly at the law school.

In the early 1970s, the Tennessee Valley Authority (TVA) began building the Tellico Dam on the Little Tennessee River in Loudon County.

Around this same time, Congress passed the Endangered Species Act of 1973, to protect wildlife that was threatened with extinction. The Act specifically prohibited federal projects that would endanger species listed by the U.S. Fish and Wildlife Service as threatened with extinction.

And guess what little fish made the endangered species list. That's right. The snail darter. And guess where the snail darter lived. Yep, in the Tennessee River on the banks of the soon-to-be Tellico Dam.

The snail darter became the interest of a UT biology professor, Dr. David Etnier, an environmental law professor, Zygmunt Plater, and a law student, Hank Hill. They submitted a petition to the Fish and Wildlife Service to determine whether the endangered snail darter was further endangered by the Tellico Dam project.

The Service investigated the situation and found that the dam would in fact interfere with a critical habitat for the snail darter, and federal funding for the project should be rescinded.

TVA responded that Congress had already spent over $100 million on the project, and inasmuch as the dam was started before the enactment of the Endangered Species Act, the Tellico Dam project should be "grandfathered" in as an exception to the Act. TVA also said the snail darter should be removed from the endangered species list.

From the perspective of the environmentally sensitive UT students and faculty, TVA was saying, "Dam the snail darter, full speed ahead!"

Law student Hank Hill, represented by Professor Plater, filed a lawsuit against TVA, seeking an injunction to stop the construction of the Tellico Dam as a violation of the Endangered Species Act.

Students and faculty members across the campus supported the lawsuit by purchasing and wearing "SAVE THE SNAIL DARTER" t-shirts.

UT President Dr. Edward Boling did not buy or wear a t-shirt. He was appalled that a UT student, represented by a UT Law professor, was suing TVA, a long-time partner of the university on many projects.

He ordered Hill and Plater to drop the lawsuit. They declined.

Dr. Boling then met with the law school Dean, Ken Penegar, and told him to order Hill and Plater to drop the lawsuit. Dean Penegar also declined, and this did not exactly lead to a good relationship between Dr. Boling and the law school.

The lawsuit proceeded and the case went all the way to the United States Supreme Court.

In 1978, in a six to three decision, the Court ruled in favor of the snail darter, or more accurately the plaintiff, law student Hank Hill. In an opinion written by Chief Justice Burger, the Court ruled that the Tellico Dam project did violate the Endangered Species Act, and had to be stopped.

T-shirt clad UT students rejoiced, and the snail darters had a big party in the Little Tennessee River.

And then Congress stepped in.

Led by Tennessee Senator Howard Baker, himself a UT Law School graduate, Congress exempted the Tellico Dam project from the Endangered Species Act.

The project was completed, but efforts to save the snail darter went on for years. TVA itself worked to transport the snail darter from the Little Tennessee River to other rivers and streams. I'm not sure how they tried to do that.

You can't bus a fish.

Environmentalists, including many UT students, supported efforts to approve water flows and increase oxygen in hundreds of miles downstream from dams.

The snail darter proved to be a feisty little creature. It was fruitful, multiplied and survived. To borrow a line from that noted Mississippi fisherman William Faulkner, the snail darter did not merely endure. It prevailed.

But there was one UT Campus protest in the 70s that unfortunately got out of hand … and almost got me kicked out of school. It was the Hess Hall Beer Bust that I hosted, and it got me busted.

Alcohol was prohibited on campus although it flowed across the campus like the Tennessee River. In our infinite wisdom or total lack thereof, SGA leaders, unfortunately including me, concluded that the policy needed to come to an official end.

And so rather than drinking behind closed doors in frat houses and dorm rooms, we organized the Hess Hall Beer Bust to be held in the courtyard of the Zoo, Hess Hall. Unfortunately, we even publicized it in *The Daily Beacon*, proudly announcing it was going to end the no alcohol policy once and for all.

A large crowd of Hess Hall residents turned out for the event. Unfortunately, so did the Campus Police. They confiscated our kegs. And then I was busted. They "wrote me up" (student conduct language for a citation) for leading the event.

And then, the following day, I received the news that the Dean of Student Conduct, Charles Burchett, wanted to have me expelled from UT for "incitement to violate university policy."

I just about wet my orange pants. I was planning on applying for law school, and it suddenly looked like I was going to need a lawyer rather than become one.

Fortunately, Chancellor Jack Reese bailed me out. He told Dean Burchett to drop his effort to make me the Abbie Hoffman of campus beer busts. And then the good Chancellor told me he thought I was an idiot.

And he was right. I never tapped a keg again. And that's my story.

From Billy Graham and Richard Nixon to the Knoxville 22, the snail darter, and the beer bust that got me busted, student activism was indeed active on the otherwise conservative campus of the University of Tennessee in the sixties and seventies.

That being said, I'm pretty sure if you mentioned the name Abbie Hoffman, the majority of the student body at the time would, first, not know who that was, and second, wonder if Abbie was either a Tri-Delt or an AOPi.

– Bill Haltom

"As much fun as I was having in college, as undecided as I was about what I was going to do with my life, an awareness was dawning in me that would define me later."

FROM KING TO KENT STATE, CHANGE BURNS IN A NATION UNDER FIRE

My freshman year, I came home to Memphis for spring break. Couple of reasons: I was dating a Memphis girl, and I didn't have any money to go anywhere. One of those things would change; I would marry Nora Ballenger my senior year, and then there were two of us without any money.

I met some friends and played golf at Galloway, a public course in Memphis. The date was March 21, 1968.

We were in shirtsleeves walking down the 17th fairway when it started to snow. The flakes were sloppy clumsy things, so big they were almost individually identifiable, the patterns almost discernable. We were laughing. By the time we putted out on the 18th, we had to sweep snow off the green to finish.

We weren't laughing; we were shivering.

That night it snowed 16+ inches, the second largest snowfall in the city's history. I somehow plowed Dad's car from my parents' house in east Memphis to Nora's parents' house in midtown. I ended up spending the night in the guest room in her father's pajamas.

That weird snow wouldn't be the marker for that spring of 1968.

That weird snow would cause the cancellation of a march led by Dr. Martin Luther King, Jr. in support of the city's striking sanitation workers.

I still wonder how the world might be different if it hadn't snowed in Memphis that day.

Two weeks later, King would be assassinated in Memphis. Two weeks later, I would stand in a dorm line for the phone trying to call home. Two weeks later, I would find all the lines to Memphis tied up, and it would take me hours to find out if my parents and Nora were all safe, if my city was on fire like so many were.

Two weeks later, my life, and my city were forever changed.

Memphis didn't burn. The brave fire fighters that made sure of it weren't with the fire department, but what they did was as brave and sure as steady hands on a hose dousing dangerous flames, as rising on ladders to reach the threat.

Black and white leaders came together as one to convince their very separate constituencies that the bullet of a madman can't be allowed to kill a city, even a dream. Memphis remains wounded even today, but the cooperation, shared vision and understanding of a relative few that saved a city 50-plus years ago remains the only true antidote that can heal us.

With that tragic event came an understanding that we have the unique responsibility to reject everything that pulled that trigger, the national events and mindsets that were behind that bullet then and now.

As much fun as I was having in college, as undecided as I was about what I was going to do with my life, an awareness was dawning in me that would define me later.

The nation was changing. I was changing.

All of that sounds as heavy as that freakish snowfall, but 1968 proved to be much heavier still. The assassination of King would be followed by the assassination of Bobby Kennedy that summer. The Democratic National Convention would explode on national television.

NEVER OVER THE HILL

I said in my foreword that college when I began in 1967 was much like college was when my father began in 1927.

We would return to campus in the fall of 1968 to longer hair, to bell bottoms and halters, to relaxed and looser styles among students if not the administration, and to the smell of a different kind of a smoke wafting from the windows of student rooms and apartments.

Even conservative UT had the munchies and a new awareness. Nixon would win the White House, but Vietnam was all the rage on campus.

A half a million people and the rock stars of an age showed up for "three days of peace and love" in a farmer's field outside of Woodstock, New York, in August of 1969. The expectations and measure of concerts changed forever. Three people died.

Like so many points of history, the people making the points of history were not aware. For instance, me. People I knew were going to Woodstock, a fling at the end of summer before school in the fall. I could do that, or go to a frat brother's wedding in Houston.

While the world paid attention to Woodstock, Calvin Ozier and I stole his father's Lincoln Continental and went to Houston.

As the fall of 1969 got rolling, Ronald Reagan pulled up to the fraternity house in a stretch limo and shook my hand. Richard Nixon didn't come to the house, but both of his daughters did. I met them, too.

Really.

My fraternity brother Max Calloway was very active in the Young Republicans at the college level nationally. Then Governor Reagan was considering a presidential run, and a stop in Knoxville, and a visit with Tennessee's favorite son, Senator Howard Baker, seemed in order. The Nixon girls showed up for the same reason.

I don't know how Max pulled it off, but all of them came to the ATO house on different occasions and spoke to the chapter in our dining room with the press in tow. I think we were supposed to represent appeal to a younger group.

All I could think about when Reagan spoke was his hosting Death Valley Days, a touch of the Gipper, and the reflection off his hair from the overhead lights. As for the Nixon girls, I thought Tricia was cuter than Julie.

I said I was changing. I didn't say that I was deeper. But that would dramatically change, too.

On December 1, 1969, the debate over whether or not one would serve in Vietnam ceased to be a grade-based question or an esoteric exercise.

The escalation of the Vietnam War was eating up young men faster than supply, so the United States held its first national draft lottery. Regardless of full-time student status or grade-point average, if your number came up, you were going to be drafted and likely sent to Vietnam.

No more student deferments.

The drawing was held on national television based on birthdays. The earlier your birthday was drawn, the more likely you were going.

Merry Christmas 1969 from Uncle Sam.

We had a lottery "party" at the frat house, more like a wake. We borrowed TVs from guys' apartments, wrapped the antennas with aluminum foil, and put them all over the house.

The guy doing the drawing on TV looked like Mr. Peeples, complete with a bad sport coat and glasses. He had a tumbler – really – a tumbler like those in a prize drawing for a raffle in the church gym – and he would spin it for each birthday, and draw your fateful number.

NEVER OVER THE HILL

For comparison purposes, my roommate Bob Alley drew number 15 and I drew number 228. He went in the Air Force National Guard. I didn't go. Pure luck.

More strings were pulled that night and the next day than all the taffy in Gatlinburg to get in every National Guard and Reserve program in the country, and much research was done on various ailments that would preclude service.

Say, heel spurs – whatever the hell they are – got one later president, Trump, out of serving, and a National Guard assignment got another later president, Bush the Son, out of serving – and there's considerable debate as to whether or not he even showed for National Guard duty.

Right after that upheaval and the Christmas break, we came back to campus to discover that a new university president, Ed Boling, had been appointed without any student notice nor involvement.

That gave student activist, Peter Kami, all he needed to raise a ruckus. He challenged Dr. Boling to hand-to-hand combat – I'm not kidding – a duel. This was to take place on The Hill in front of the administration building on January 15.

About 200 core protestors and 1,000 spectators showed up – including me. Dr. Boling did not.

Kami called for a rush to enter the administration building. The UT police were present in force and were soon backed up by Knoxville police. In the melee that followed, seven protestors and four police were injured. Kami and 21 others were arrested and dubbed the Knoxville 22.

Any UT student who has had occasion to be confronted by both campus police and UT police – ahem – will tell you to run towards the UT police. Knoxville cops consider it a career highlight to arrest a UT student.

When I turned toward the administration building as the crowd moved that way, I found myself facing one of Knoxville's finest in some sort of helmet.

He greeted me with a swing of the billy club he had in his hand, but he telegraphed it with a grunt – he was a round sort of guy – so I ducked, caught part of it on the shoulder, and took off. Not looking back, I dove into a big bush thinking I'd lose him in the confusion.

I was right. But it was a thorn bush. Tore me up like a cheese shredder. When I got back to the house bleeding and with a sore shoulder, I enjoyed some small celebrity.

I was the Thorn Bush One.

That spring quarter, National Guardsmen fired on unarmed student protestors at Kent State University. Suddenly, my thorn bush moment wasn't funny anymore.

That was May 4, 1970. Four unarmed students were killed. Nine other unarmed students were wounded. It became known as the Kent State Massacre.

A week or so later, I was pulling an all-nighter for an exam in the living room of the frat house. There was one other brother in there doing the same.

If you've ever taken an amphetamine – we called them Black Widows, $1 a pill – you know that you can memorize War & Peace in one night, but you won't remember any of it by lunch the next day, so timing is important. Even more important, you *do not engage anyone in a conversation while under the influence, because you can't stop talking.*

The other guy – as I said – the only other guy in the room and I started talking. We didn't stop for ten hours. We both knew better, but the subject was Kent State.

NEVER OVER THE HILL

That's when I got serious about getting serious. I credit that night in setting a direction for me, drawing a line for me. About the power of power. About the result of too much, or none. About the result of rationalization and the cost.

About questioning instead of just accepting. Always.

The other guy was Jay Anania, a year younger than me. We weren't arguing. We were agreeing, and building on that agreement, challenging, and exploring.

Discovering who we were.

I'm pretty sure of two things: we both blew the exams, and we both remember the marathon discussion, even though we were wired, we remember.

Jay went on to a very distinguished career as a filmmaker, screenwriter, and director, including directing the graduate program of the film school at NYU. Here's what the Museum of Modern Art (MoMA) in New York had to say about Jay on the occasion of the world premiere of his film *One Morning in 1904* at the museum in 2021.

"Born in Maryland and based in New York, Jay Anania is that most independent of filmmakers who, for the past five decades, has written, directed, shot, and edited features and documentaries with the sparest of means but the most expansive of formal ambitions. His work is as exquisitely attuned to the play of light or passage of time on a landscape as it is to an actor's spontaneous gesture or poetic turn of phrase."

So there. I could have told them he was a pretty interesting guy to talk to all night.

His baby sister was the late Elizabeth Anania Edwards, the brave and embattled wife of disgraced North Carolina Senator and presidential candidate, John Edwards.

College should challenge you, charge you, change you. Thorns and all. If one ends just as one begins, one has to wonder, what did it matter?

– Dan Conaway

"But there was one speaker the Issues committee invited that the UT administration did not want us students to hear. He wasn't a politician or a sex therapist. He was a comedian."

THE OPEN CAMPUS CONTROVERSY: FREE SPEECH ON THE HILL

It was called the Issues series.

Each year a number of nationally prominent Americans would come to the UT Knoxville campus to lecture on issues ranging from politics to literature to entertainment to sexuality. They were selected and invited by the student-run Issues committee.

The speakers I heard during my era at UT included United States Supreme Court Justice William O. Douglas, Presidential historian Arthur Schlesinger, urban sociologist Jane Jacobs, and behavioral psychologist B.F. Skinner. Author Tom Wolfe appeared in his trademark white suit after the publication of his counterculture classic, "The Electric Kool Aid Acid Test."

While there was no "Sex Week" at UT in the 70s, two of the most popular Issues speakers were the research team of Masters and Johnson, co-authors of the best-selling "Human Sexual Response." They appeared before a capacity crowd at Alumni Gym, walking on stage hand-in-hand to an ovation usually reserved for Vol touchdowns at Neyland Stadium.

"The topic sells, "observed William Masters at the beginning of his lecture with Virginia Johnson.

But there was one speaker the Issues committee invited that the UT administration did not want us students to hear. He wasn't a politician or a sex therapist. He was a comedian.

His name was Dick Gregory.

Gregory was not your typical stand-up comedian. He was an outspoken African American who poked fun at racism and bigotry in graphic no-holds barred routines. A typical line in his stand-up: "I walked into a restaurant in the south. A white waitress came up to me and said, 'We don't serve colored people here.' I said, 'That's all right. I don't eat colored people. Bring me some fried chicken!'"

Such routines, as well as his strong opposition to the Vietnam War, won Gregory millions of fans, but many detractors as well. One of those who was not a fan of Gregory was UT Chancellor Charles Weaver. He called Gregory "an extreme racist … whose appearance would be an outrage and an insult to many citizens of (Tennessee)."

He revoked Gregory's invitation by the Issues committee to speak on the campus. This led to the "Open Campus" controversy.

SGA President Chris Whittle, who would after his graduation from UT become the Editor and Publisher of Esquire magazine and the developer of numerous other media enterprises, organized a speaker policy rally on campus, calling for an "open campus." He argued that the issue was not whether Dick Gregory should be invited and allowed to speak on campus. At stake, he said, was "the very meaning of a university education in a democratic society."

The Student Government issued a "Statement of Principle," declaring if students came to UT only to "develop technical skills" or to "memorize a given set of facts in a subject area," then the traditional classroom served that purpose. But if the goal was "to encourage students in the development of full civic and social participation, and beyond that to educate the whole man," the UT Administration should be "encouraging students to tap the intellectual resources of whomever they wish to hear and believe they could benefit from."

The Chancellor was clearly worried that an appearance by Gregory would provoke a hostile reaction by Tennessee legislators. He refused to rescind his cancellation of the invitation to Gregory, and referred the matter to the University's Board of Trustees for an "in-depth study."

The Board of Trustees responded by announcing a campus speakers policy whereby the university administration could decide which campus events were in "the students' best interests," and cancel those that were not.

A number of students and faculty members—calling themselves the "Open Campus Coalition"—then sued the University, claiming that the administration's cancellation of the invitation to Dick Gregory and its "best interests of the students" speaker policy violated the First Amendment.

On April 14, 1969, UT students and faculty members packed the courtroom of the United States District Court for the Eastern District of Tennessee. There they heard another controversial speaker, famed ACLU attorney William Kunstler. He had previously represented Martin Luther King, Jr., Stokely Carmichael, Lenny Bruce and the Chicago Seven, arguing for their First Amendment rights.

Now he argued to Federal District Judge Robert Taylor that the University's speaker policy violated the First Amendment in its position that the University could decide which campus events were in the students' best interest, "a clause so vague it gave administrators unlimited power to keep controversial speakers off campus."

The University's attorney argued that the University promoted diverse viewpoints, but had no obligation to host any particular speaker. He said that students were not being deprived of their First Amendment rights "even though they might not get the speaker of their choice."

Judge Taylor ruled in favor of the "open campus" coalition. He found UT's speaker policy denied the UT students' rights to "receive information and ideas."

NEVER OVER THE HILL

One year later, on April 9, 1970 – two years after his initial invitation – Dick Gregory appeared on the UT campus and spoke to a capacity crowd of 4,000 in Alumni Gym. The speech was well-received.

UT had indeed become an open campus. And even Chancellor Weaver embraced it.

Just one month after Dick Gregory's long delayed speech, famed evangelist Billy Graham arrived in Knoxville to hold a crusade on campus at Neyland Stadium. As noted earlier herein, Graham announced that a featured speaker at the crusade would be President Richard Nixon.

When a number of students and faculty members objected to the appearance of Reverend Graham and the President to speak at the University's football stadium, Chancellor Weaver said he had no choice in the matter.

With a smile on his face, he said giving Reverend Graham and the President a platform in Neyland Stadium "demonstrates the essential correctness of our open speaker policy."

Yep.

– Bill Haltom

*"About 4,000 students voted, and
I emerged from a crowded field with
the most counted votes. Before I could give
my victory speech, Albert Ailor gave
his own, claiming a landslide win
of 21,000 non-votes!"*

SGA: GOVERNMENT OF THE STUDENTS, BY THE STUDENTS, AND FOR THE STUDENTS

During Spring Quarter of my sophomore year, I decided to enter politics.

I threw my orange hat in the ring and ran for the Student Senate. I was elected, and I took my seat in the Capitol, otherwise known as the large conference room in the student center.

The UT Student Senate was just one step above student council. Actually. It wasn't a step above student council. It WAS student council.

We passed lots of resolutions in the Student Senate…resolutions calling for an end to the Vietnam War, the legalization of marijuana, and all sorts of liberal causes even though the UT student body was quite conservative. The joke around the campus at the time was that the Student Senate was "for acid, amnesty and abortion," although I do not recall Student Senator Haltom supporting even two out of three. Maybe one.

The resolutions had no impact whatsoever in the non-academic real world. I am confident that in the White House Oval Office, President Nixon never asked Haldeman or Erhlichman, "What does the University of Tennessee Student Senate say about this issue?"

At least I never heard anything like that on the White House tapes that were released after the Watergate investigation.

The most controversial resolution the student senate passed during that era did not involve a political issue. So help me, it involved the song "Dixie."

CONAWAY AND HALTOM

The Ole Miss football team was scheduled to play our Volunteers in Neyland Stadium in November of 1972, and we student senators heard they were bringing their band. In those days the Ole Miss band played "Dixie" as often as the Pride of the Southland would come to play "Rocky Top."

Our Volunteers football team included the SEC's first Black quarterback, Condredge Holloway, and other outstanding Black players. None of them indicated they would be offended by hearing the Ole Miss band play the song about the land of cotton where old times there were not forgotten.

But we members of the UT Student Senate would not look away.

We unanimously passed a resolution calling for the Ole Miss band to refrain from playing "Dixie" in Neyland Stadium, and sent it to the President of the student body at the University of Mississippi. It was not well-received. The Ole Miss Student Government responded with its own resolution telling us to mind our own orange business.

On November 18, 1972, the Ole Miss band came to Neyland Stadium and pretty much played "Dixie" non-stop through four quarters.

Condredge Holloway responded with something much more effective than resolutions. He led the Vols to a 17-0 shutout of the Rebels.

But the Student Senate did more than pass ineffectual resolutions. We actually tried to do some meaningful things, such as registering students to vote, not in student government elections, but in elections for President, Governor, Senators (ones in Washington, not the student center), representatives, mayors, and dog catchers.

In 1971, the 26th Amendment to the United States Constitution was ratified, lowering the voting age to 18. The Student Senate launched a campus-wide campaign to register students to vote.

We asked the Knox County Election Commission to set up voter registration tables at the student center.

Our request was declined.

We then organized groups of students to go to the election commission offices and register to vote. But the county election commission refused to register UT students unless they were residents of Knox County. We could not claim our dormitory, off-campus apartment, or frat house as our domicile.

I tried to register claiming my residency to be my post office box at the student center. In rejecting my application, the election commission official told me, "You're little, but you can't live in no post office box."

We then collected mail order voting applications and distributed them around the campus, encouraging students to register to vote wherever they lived in the Volunteer State.

The following year, during Spring Quarter 1973, I again ran for office. I was elected Student Government Association President, although there was some controversy about whether I had won.

One of my main opponents in the election was my friend Albert Ailor. He ran on what he called the "Apathy Ticket," claiming student government was a joke. He urged students to not vote for him or me or anyone in student elections.

Of the 25,000 students at UT in the spring of 1973, most heeded the call of Albert Apathy Ailor, assuming they even heard it. About 4,000 students voted, and I emerged from a crowded field with the most counted votes. Before I could give my victory speech, Albert Ailor gave his own, claiming a landslide win of 21,000 non-votes!

But the student election commission certified me as the winner, and I served as President of the UT Student Government at the same to Richard Nixon was President of the United States. Unlike President Nixon, I did not install a taping system in the SGA offices in the student center, so I was never forced to resign in disgrace.

As SGA President, I worked with the Student Senate on two main issues, neither of which involving acid, amnesty, or abortion.

The first was allowing alcohol on campus where it was strictly prohibited, although enforcement was limited and selective. Beer and booze pretty much flowed in frat houses, but not in residence halls. We petitioned the Board of Trustees to reverse the policy, and even announced plans to open a Rathskeller in the student center if and when the policy was changed.

The Board of Trustees unanimously rejected our request, voting to keep the UT campus dry, even though beer rained in many spots on campus.

I then made the mistake of organizing an act of student civil disobedience, a beer bust in the courtyard of Hess Hall. As you can read in another chapter, UT Safety and Security stopped this event, confiscated the beers kegs, and wrote me up for violating campus policy.

Dean of Student Conduct Burchett wanted to expel me, but fortunately for me, Chancellor Jack Reese awarded me amnesty!

The other issue for the Haltom SGA Administration had a happier outcome. We worked to get a student on the Board of Trustees. This required action by the Tennessee Legislature.

The UT Administration opposed this, but the SGA organized trips to Nashville where students lobbied legislators to support our cause. To the surprise of the UT Administration, we won the support of then House Speaker and future Governor Ned McWherter and Lt. Governor John Wilder.

NEVER OVER THE HILL

On the day the issue came to a vote in the legislature, we students packed galleries of the Tennessee House and Senate. I remember that one of our supporters, Representative Tommy Burnett, made a strong speech just before the vote. He pointed to us students in the gallery, and said, "Look at these fine young people! All you see on TV are hippies and protesters! But these young people are real representatives of the students in our state! They deserve representation on our University's Board of Trustees!"

Fortunately, he did not mention the recent Hess Hall beer bust.

The Tennessee Senate and House overwhelmingly voted to create a student position on the Board of Trustees. And shortly thereafter, we students gathered in the offices of Governor Winfield Dunn as he signed the Act giving students representation on the trustee board.

I left the SGA Oval Office (actually a rectangular one) in the Spring of 1973, and never ran for public office again.

My political career ended with the Hess Hall beer bust, and a student on the Boards of Trustees.

I'll drink to that.

– Bill Haltom

SIDE HUSTLES

What makes us who we are is the application,
and the testing,
of what we heard in the classroom out in the world.

We discover ourselves out there.

*"We were no threat, because they knew
I was going back to college and that
Charles was going nowhere."*

BUILDING NEW BOXES

Your first job in a box plant, you learn things.

The summer after my freshman year back home in Memphis, I learned more about life and circumstance, about systemic racism, and about hard-earned money than I would at UT in four years.

Those lessons have lasted a lifetime.

You learn how to suck smoke a cigarette in a minute or less since stopping to do it is holding up production. You learn that bathrooms are for designated break times since stopping to do it is holding up production.

You learn about boxes. And bigger things.

"Listen here, college boy. Bend your knees when you pick that up, or you won't make a week."

That sound advice came from Charles, across a huge stack of corrugated boards that would soon hold refrigerators, on my first day at Mead Container in Memphis. Way over on Manassas, north of Chelsea, way down in a predominantly Black area of town, a predominantly poor area of town, way far away from my East Memphis house in miles and mindsets.

For me, it was the first day in a job that would last the summer after my freshman year. For Charles, it was another day on a job he just hoped would last.

That day, that summer, I learned a lot.

I learned that a box that will hold a refrigerator is roughly the size of a dorm room when flat, that the edges of a corrugated box will turn hands

223

into hamburger, that my new name was college boy, and that the difference between Black and white – between my expectations and those of my fellow laborers – was Black and white.

It wasn't that all the laborers on the plant floor, with my lily-white exception, were Black, and that the holders of every position above that, with no exceptions, were white. That wasn't subtle. Charles and I loaded flat boxes on conveyors leading to tall finishing machines operated by white folks who were literally above us and literally talked down to us.

It was the equality of the inequality, the steady repression of ambition. Those machine operators, the next step up, made sure we stayed down there where we belonged. We were no threat, because they knew I was going back to college and that Charles was going nowhere.

I had no idea what I'd end up doing, but I knew it wasn't that, and I had been taught that my only limitation would be me. Charles only had one ambition – to drive the forklift. That was the highest hourly wage job on the floor, and he knew his limits.

With that limited knowledge, the people who operate machines win.

"Think outside the box." I truly hate that cliché. Creativity "outside the box" without purpose, direction or measure is intellectual masturbation. Real creativity challenges conceits, alters perception, expands the possible, changes reality. Real creativity solves real problems.

Real creativity builds new boxes.

Some of us are in boxes that have no more room for change, no seat for the different, no greater ambition than to keep what we have – even worse – to go back and get something we think we had. Boxes like this are destined for attics.

So many of us are trapped in the box of not just the unemployed, but the underemployed – the soul-draining existence people endure knowing they're better than that. Boxes like this explode.

We need new boxes big enough to hold and nurture greater dreams than Charles had, big enough that all of us will need to bend our knees together to pick it up.

Small ideas, small minds come in small, closed boxes.

That first summer in college I learned why I was in college, and that I had much to learn in and out of classrooms.

I know from boxes.

– Dan Conaway

NEVER OVER THE HILL

"I wanted to be either a Beacon paper boy or columnist. There were no jobs in the former, and so I got the latter."

THE DAILY BEACON AND OTHER WRITE STUFF

UT was a big orange sandbox for me.

I got to be a sandbox politician running for the Student Senate and even being elected SGA President. I was a sandbox radio host with my own weekly talk show on the campus station, WUOT.

But the coolest thing I got to be at UT was a sandbox journalist, as I became a columnist for the UT Daily Beacon.

And what a great sandbox it was! The Beacon was published five days a week and had a circulation of 25,000 given the fact that it was available to every student on campus.

Writing for the Beacon was my second job in journalism. Starting in the sixth grade, I worked in circulation for the Memphis Press Scimitar. I was a paper boy.

But at UT, I went from throwing a newspaper to writing for one. I took a major cut in pay. As a paper boy I made about $20 a week, which was a lot of money in the sixth grade. As a columnist for the Beacon I was paid, well, nothing, but it was great fun working in the Beacon newsroom in the College of Communications.

The Beacon ran my column every Thursday, and God forgive me, but I loved seeing my byline. I put the vanity in vanity press.

On my Beacon platform, I pontificated on campus issues, but mostly I had fun turning out what purported to be humor columns. I was no Lewis Grizzard, but some of my fellow students said my columns made them laugh. To this day, it is about the nicest compliment I've ever received.

NEVER OVER THE HILL

And how did I get this wonderful gig as a columnist?

I would like to tell you I won a campus-wide writing competition. I would like to say that the great Kelly Leiter, Dean of the College of Communications, saw my talent and urged me to write for the Beacon.

But as Woody Allen famously said, ninety percent of success consists of showing up.

And that's what I did. I walked into the Beacon office one day, introduced myself to the editors and writers, including Wendell Potter and Joan Lollar and Charlotte Durham and Paula Casey (just to name a few), and said I wanted to be either a Beacon paper boy or columnist. There were no jobs in the former, and so I got the latter.

This was one of the great things about UT. You could go climb into any sandbox on the campus doing some fun things.

My days as a non-paid columnist for the Beacon led to a part-time poorly paid career as a columnist for the Tennessean, the Knoxville News Sentinel, the Commercial Appeal, and other newspapers. But alas, I never did get back into the lucrative job as a paper boy!

And here's the best part. Look right below this sentence. Yep, that's my byline.

– Bill Haltom

"There was no medal ceremony, and nobody wanted to hear the alma mater, so I just hummed it."

SHOOTING THE MOON FOR GOLD

When the Olympics roll around, my fellow decathlete, Jeff Chamblin, and I have laughed our way through the memories, remembering the competition as if it were yesterday.

We remember the wedge on 18 at Galloway Golf Course, dug from a heavy lie in a front yard on Walnut Grove Road, arriving there after a 350-yard drive, 250 yards of that bouncing in the street. Even now, we can see the wedge rising over five lanes of traffic. We can hear the horns, the homeowner scream from his porch, as we watch that scarred, bruised warrior of a ball hit, bounce and bite to eight feet for birdie. Don't tell me about the troublesome rules of golf. In this competition, if you could find it and hit it, it was in play, and that was a helluva shot.

We all gasped when top right English sent the three across the table into the money ball dropping it in the corner pocket. We couldn't believe it when the backhand slam from somewhere out in the driveway sent the opponent diving into the corner of the carport as a ping pong ball and his medal chances whizzed by his ear.

In the middle of several Olympics since, the Memphis Olympics in the middle of 1970 have come to mind.

That summer, ten competitors gathered for the event. A number of colleges were represented – none, I assure you, officially. The University of Memphis, then Memphis State, had several representatives including Jeff. Somebody from Southwestern, later Rhodes College, a couple from Ole Miss – a couple between, let's say, college opportunities. I, of course, was the sole University of Tennessee designee, designated, of course, by me.

I was taking summer school courses at night at the Goodman Institute Building in downtown Memphis which gave course credit at both UT and Memphis State, so there might have been some dual eligibility issues.

I can't remember everybody, but I remember the games.

Jeff and I worked for *The Commercial Appeal* that summer and while we were supposed to be selling ads one afternoon, we were doing something more rewarding – drinking beer and coming up with a decathlon of the games we grew up playing – a sort of east Memphis upbringing Olympiad.

Horse was in, Around The World was out, because Horse is more creative since you don't shoot from fixed positions. Another beer. Poker and Hearts were in, but Bridge was out since a partner is required. Monopoly was on board, but Parcheesi was, well, too cheesy. Another beer. Leftfield ball and bowling would be the team sports. And so on. And another beer.

Ten competitors. Ten events over the weekend. Bowling, Leftfield Ball, Horse, 9-Ball, Golf, Tennis, Poker, Ping Pong, Monopoly, Hearts.

We remember all that, but we can't remember everybody who competed, or what we competed for – beer and money to be sure, but we're not sure how much. Jeff claims he took the gold, but I know better.

In the last event – Hearts – I was hoarding the ace and queen of hearts, and when I took Jeff's king with that ace, I shot the moon and used the 26 points to take him and the gold.

There was no medal ceremony, and nobody wanted to hear the alma mater, so I just hummed it.

That's what I remember. I think.

Just games, but games can bring out the best and worst in us, show us some of our brightest and darkest moments, stir old memories, and cause belly laughs between two old friends on the phone. That's pure gold.

I love the Olympics, and I'm still waiting for my medal from UT.

– Dan Conaway

"Ladies and gentlemen, I seem to have forgotten my entire presentation," I said. "Please enjoy your desserts and I'll be with you when it all returns."

THE COMPETITION YOU'VE NEVER HEARD OF: AND WE WON IT ALL, AND I FORGOT IT ALL

Dick Joel was the advertising department head when I was a senior, and you could get most of the graduating advertising majors in a single classroom.

The College of Communications was still a baby, and only one or two graduating classes had gone out into the world from UT with degrees in communications in any of the then disciplines: journalism, broadcasting, public relations, and advertising.

The brand-new home of the college was a half-circle building shaped around one side of Circle Park across from the McClung Museum behind the new Torchbearer statue. The sleek building housed the college radio station, The Daily Beacon student newspaper, and the Tennessee Newspaper Hall of Fame, overlooking, and looking up to, Neyland Stadium.

I was in there, too. And I thought it was the coolest place on Earth.

Professor Joel had been advertising department head at Florida State and he had been heavily recruited by the new college dean Don Hileman to build the advertising department.

He took what he had to work with and whipped us into shape. His black suit and tie couldn't hide the fact that he looked a bit like an elf – a senior white-haired elf.

Out of his seniors, he recruited a team to represent the College of Communications and the University of Tennessee in the American Advertising Federation Student Advertising Competition.

NEVER OVER THE HILL

The AAF started the competition in their 7th Deep South District in the late 60s inviting colleges in eight or nine southern states to participate. Professor Joel had teams at Florida State, but discovered that Tennessee had yet to compete.

His pitch was really compelling: you'll do this in addition to your regular assignments, you'll get no extra credit, you'll have no budget, you'll have very little time, and, while he would be our advisor, he couldn't actually write a word of our presentation or edit it in any way.

And, oh, he added, the University of Georgia has already been working on this for two months, they do have a budget, and they've won the last two of these competitions.

Go, team.

Turns out, much of that kind of pressure, that kind of dependence on each other, and no second place or trophies for participation would be more like what we'd face after graduation than any classroom experience could provide.

We were late getting started, but we had a good bunch. We had about five weeks.

John Bryant was a Vietnam vet. Lt. Bryant has led his men into jungle combat. He wasn't going to blink in the face of an advertising deadline. Carolyn Stone was as smooth in presentation as 20-year-old whiskey. Beth Browning was as good with numbers as Texas Instruments and almost as quick. Ashleigh Groce was as tough as John and as demanding as Joel. My job was to write copy and make us laugh when nothing was funny. I was – and am – pretty good at those things.

All the schools had the same hypothetical assignment and budget: introducing a new facial tissue in several colors that was rapidly biodegradable.

We named it Mirage and had a sheik as spokesperson – try that today.

The competition was in Columbus – Georgia, not Ohio – over a couple of days. The judges were all from national ad agencies. You may have even heard of some of these – J. Walter Thompson, McCann Erickson, BBD&O, Doyle Dane Bernbach – okay, okay, so you haven't heard of them, but in our world, they were giants.

You couldn't see the competition just like you can't watch your competitors pitch in the real world. The aforementioned Georgia presented right before us to the same judges.

As we got going, we couldn't help but notice that the guy from J. Walter Thompson kept shaking his head. So much so, I wanted to say, "Hey, pal, if it bothers you that much just leave."

That would have gone over well.

When it was over, we were pretty sure it was over for us. After a couple of hours of feeling sorry for ourselves, all the competitors were called into a big room with all the judges sitting at a table up front.

Everyone was thanked. The guy from Thompson took the mike to announce the winner. As he described how impressed he was with every aspect of the presentation, he stared shaking his head.

I looked at Joel. He was tearing up – over an advertising competition. I loved that man. Seriously, I loved him.

Georgia knew. Joel knew. We knew. Everybody knew. We had won.

All these decades later, the little wood and brass plaque that each of us won stands on a bookcase next to a black-and-white photograph of the team. John Bryant – the jungle war veteran – has a grin on his face that makes him look like he's about 14 years old, a very large 14 years old.. Dick Joel is in his signature black suit, smiling and proving that elves can inspire magic. Carolyn's and Ashleigh's and Beth's dresses are ridiculous short, and I'm in the back in a gray rubber suit – the fabric was all the rage – double-knit – and a ridiculously wide tie.

I've won a lot of stuff over the years and received a lot of statues and accolades. None are more important than that plaque and pic to remind me of that seminal spring and those people.

The competition went national three years later in 1974. Now, more than 2,000 students participate each year. Our daughter and son were on teams their senior years at Tennessee in 1997 and 2003 respectively.

About three weeks after Columbia, our team was invited to present our winning pitch at the AAF Seventh District Convention in Birmingham. We were the banquet program the last night.

As they had for the competition, the other team members presented their portions on slides. As in the competition, I would present the creative on boards, standing next to an easel fashioned by me to look like a huge sheik holding the boards, and with an audio tape for the radio – to be played through the hotel speakers.

I was the big finish. Right out there in the middle of the banquet hall, literally in a spotlight.

As a reached to reveal the first board, I went blank. Clueless. Nobody home.

After writing every word of this, after drawing the sheik and voicing his part in the radio spots, after rehearsing all of this a zillion times, after presenting it in competition, I was standing right out there in the middle of 500 people, all looking at me, and I had absolutely nothing.

I could've cried, but then I would still be standing there. And crying.

"Ladies and gentlemen, I seem to have forgotten my entire presentation," I said. "Please enjoy your desserts and I'll be with you when it all returns."

There were gasps – some of the guests, my team, Professor Joel – some laughter, and then nervous rattling of forks digging into cheesecake while this kid was dying.

About a week later, probably two minutes, I remembered my opening, and everything else followed.

Afterwards, there was a party on the hotel roof. A man came up to me, introduced himself as Dave Swearingen, principal of an ad agency in Memphis.

He offered me a job. I was newly married and without one of those. They come in handy.

He told me, "I was impressed with what you presented, but I was more impressed by your recovery."

I would later become his partner in the ad agency Swearingen & Conaway.

If you'd known Dave, you would have known that there were a number of colorful adjectives thrown in to what he told me that I didn't include, and that he handed me a drink when he said it, but you get the point.

Believe in it, and in yourself, and stick with it.

You can beat Georgia, and anybody else, like that.

– *Dan Conaway*

The winning team included: Professor Dick Joel, Carolyn Stone, John Bryant, Beth Browning, Dan Conaway and Ashleigh Groce.

VFL AND FFL

If when you leave UT, you don't
have a big piece of it in your DNA,
if people you met there aren't still in your life,
then you simply weren't paying attention.

"Richard also raised iguanas in Hess Hall. His dorm room looked like it was infested by baby dinosaurs."

A RHODES SCHOLAR, ROADS SCHOLARS, AND A HOST OF VOLUNTEERS

When I arrived at the University of Tennessee in September of 1970, there were 25,000 students enrolled on The Hill. I didn't meet them all, but I met dorms-full, frat houses-full, sororities-full, classes-full, and few thousand in the student section of Neyland Stadium on autumn Saturday afternoons.

Many of these Vols for Life became my Friends for Life, and one of them volunteered or agreed to be the love of my life.

My VFL-FFLs included scholars such as Nancy-Ann Min. She was from Rockwood, Tennessee. John Ward called Vol fullback. Curt Watson who was from Crossville, Tennessee, "the Crossville Comet." Chancellor Jack Reese called Nancy-Ann "the Rockwood Rocket." And she deserved the moniker.

Nancy-Ann was the first female President of the SGA. She graduated Phi Beta Kappa with a perfect 4.0 and won a Rhodes Scholarship.

When I heard she was going to graduate school in Oxford, I congratulated her for winning a scholarship to Ole Miss. After attending the other Oxford, which has no football team, she went to law school at Harvard which I understand is an accredited university in Massachusetts.

She went on to a fabulous career in law and public affairs, serving as the White House Director of Health Reform during the Obama Administration.

NEVER OVER THE HILL

Other scholars included my freshman year roommate, Glen Reed, who graduated number one in the College of Liberal Arts. I was right behind him pulling up the rear.

Pam Reeves led the Academic Council and even had time to take joy rides with down Cumberland Avenue in a laundry cart. (See the chapter on unofficial extracurricular activities.)

She later became the first female judge and chief judge of the federal court for East Tennessee.

Janet Wright was President of Delta Delta Delta and a true scholar. She went on to medical school, a fabulous career as a cardiovascular surgeon, and served as Director of Science and Policy for the Surgeon General.

I was a Rhodes Scholar myself, or rather a Roads Scholar, as I packed many of by VFL-FFLs in my 1968 VW Beetle and drove us to the Smokies for hikes, or all the way to Florida for spring break. And, as previously mentioned, I rode in a laundry card down a road or rather Avenue called Cumberland.

Other orange colleagues were successful politicians, and not just in campus politics.

While in law school, SGA President Karl Schledwitz managed the successful campaign of Jim Sasser for the United States Senate.

Bob Schiffer, who somehow found his way to UT from Brooklyn, New York, worked in Congressional and gubernatorial campaigns across the country, and went on to work in the White House, developing America's first trade agreement with Vietnam.

Other VFL-FFLs of mine did some really creative stuff.

Richard Toussaint created a re-cycling system for the entire campus. Glass (beer bottles), and aluminum (beer cans) were deposited in black and yellow bins, and green computer paper was collected at the computer labs at Glocker Hall. It was an incredible recycling system ahead of its time.

Richard also raised iguanas in Hess Hall. His dorm room looked like it was infested by baby dinosaurs.

Loretta Harber and Billy Nolan worked and lobbied in the Tennessee legislature for a new Landlord-Tenant law that outlined the rights and obligations of both landlords and tenants, assisting students who lived off campus in Fort Sanders.

They also successfully lobbied the legislature to get a student on the UT Board of Trustees.

And I actually taught a class called "Philosophy of Marx…Groucho!" It was held one night a week at the student center. The class watched classic Marx Brothers movies. It offered absolutely no academic credit but was great fun.

My VFL-FFLs were indeed Volunteers, and in their work both in and outside the classroom, they exemplified the spirit of The Hill.

Unforgettable.

– Bill Haltom

"We all met at the University of Tennessee. We learned many things. Some of them actually led to degrees. Sometimes I wonder how we all graduated. All the time, actually."

FOUND, NOT LOST

I once met Bob Hope.

He was appearing on campus and my roommate and I thought it might be a good idea to make him an honorary member of our frat. Why? Well, we'd heard his son was an ATO at Arizona. And I was the public information officer for the chapter. And we'd had a lot of beer. And ... aw, what the hell ... so we climbed a fire escape and through the window into the hall of a hotel and knocked on his suite door.

Amazingly, he came to the door. I gave him my pin and he graciously accepted it and shut the door.

It never occurred to either of us to bring a camera, or that I would never see my pin again, or that absolutely no one would believe us, or that drunk is no way to climb a fire escape.

But Bob and I had that memory. Not Bob Hope, the honorary ATO, but Bob Alley, the roommate.

Hope's theme song, "Thanks For The Memory," is all too appropriate.

The memory of a 17-year-old kid from Florida who had never seen snow, and when he did see it way up on a mountain on our ATO pledge retreat at Tuckaleechee, he stole the faculty advisor's car, drove as far up there as he could, and walked the rest of the way to play in it.

The memory of him taking me for a cup of coffee at Dunkin' Donuts in Fort Lauderdale. In his plane. Flying low over Miami Beach just after dawn, and so low over the Everglades you felt you could reach out and touch the waving sea of grass. We laughed a lot.

In 2012, I delivered a eulogy for Bob Alley. Fraternity brother, college roommate, best friend.

Maybe you believe that connections like that are never broken, and become permanent residents in a greater eternal consciousness. Or maybe, upon reading that last sentence, you'd say what Bob would, "Oh, please."

NEVER OVER THE HILL

But I believe this: we don't lose people like that, we gain from having known them, we grow from the experiences shared, we own the memories, and we know we were and can be special markers in the lives of others, parts of other families, parts, in fact, of other people.

When they go, unfairly young or fairly relieved of pain, a part of us goes as well.

We can take comfort in what remains. In the things you think of – in family and friends still here, in the twinkle in a baby's eye and a new ripple in the gene pool – but also in long-familiar things you might not think about much.

And be thankful for the whole ride.

In late spring, some of us who started that ride together in Knoxville decades ago get together and fire up the engines again. I'm thankful that we can laugh so hard at stories from a lifetime ago that they still brighten the lifetime lived since.

Bob's not there, but, of course, Bob is there.

As I write this, I'm alone in the kitchen of an old friend, David Sims, in Wilmington, North Carolina.

Well, I'm not quite alone. My dogs are here, too, and a big Golden Retriever. So far, he's putting up with my two dogs just fine. Over the top of my cup of coffee and out there past the porch, a gentle wind is moving the Spanish moss on the live oaks, and the water out in the marsh and creek beyond.

I still can't get used to Spanish moss in North Carolina, but that's the magic of the Gulf Stream.

There's a boat out there we'll all be on later, roaring down the Intracoastal Waterway, holding cold beers, frying every inch of old skin exposed to the sun, and pretending we're a lot younger, and that it didn't hurt getting on and off that boat.

That's magic, too.

I have lots of memories of the old friends still asleep in this house, and about some not here this time. But, of course, Bob is here, whispering to me. And he'll join all of us on that boat later today.

We all met at the University of Tennessee. We learned many things. Some of them actually led to degrees. Sometimes I wonder how we all graduated. All the time, actually.

As I'll look around the lunch table here later today, many tables over many years, I'll again be thankful for those I still see, thankful for those I'll always remember.

Thankful that the same old guys can still bring each other to tears, laughing so hard at the same old stories from a lifetime ago that they still brighten the lifetime lived since.

Thankful for the women I see, seen even back then, putting up with us, loving us, despite real knowledge of the reality of us over all those years.

Let's review but a few examples.

Steve Larkin said good night to his date at her dorm, and pinched a Reader's Digest on the way out the door to read on his walk back to the frat house.

How close you have to hold the page to your face, and how hard you have to stare in order to read it in the dark between streetlights might have been a factor in what happened next.

NEVER OVER THE HILL

He took a shortcut through a university construction site, now trying to read by moonlight, and stepped right over the edge of a pit – a hole 15 feet across and 15 feet deep – and broke his pelvis upon arriving at the bottom. He climbed out of the hole, somehow finished the walk to the frat house, and asked for a ride to the ER – assuring his place in legend.

The owner of this house, David Sims, was at the wheel of a legendary flight.

His passengers and metal screamed, in-flight drinks and oil spilled, and only moonlight lit the ground below. There were no wings, no landing gear on this troubled, star-crossed craft, but one of those I still see across the table was the pilot, and he brought it safely down and all walked away.

He didn't, however, keep the chili cheese dogs safely down, and his date kept walking.

After all, David had just launched a p.o.s. butt-ugly Mercury Comet off a barricade and taken it airborne 100 feet across Alcoa Highway and into frat history.

This same Captain Comet later took the grapes from my backyard fence in Memphis and tried to make wine, blowing up the batch in his kitchen and covering every square inch of every surface, and one dog, with pale red splatter.

One of his passengers, Kenny Clayton, currently snoring upstairs, made sure of David's place in history by screaming, "We all almost died!", upon his return to the frat house and telling the story of the fateful Comet flight.

Kenny himself has history as well.

I believe he still holds the unofficial UT Shot Down in Flames Award for most unsuccessful phone calls trying to land a date. The final was 27 calls on the fraternity house phone. At number six, a betting pool started, and a crowd formed. I'm sure #27 wondered why she heard so much cheering and applause in the background.

King Rogers is here, too.

King once decided to take a nap following a big game. In his plate of ribs. In front of six couples. If I hadn't turned his head to the side, I'm pretty sure he would have drowned in the sauce. Come to think of it, even though I ate his ribs while he marinated, I've never been properly thanked for saving his life.

To his credit, he sponged off with 16 or so wet wipes and rallied for the remainder of the night. To his further credit, he would later serve as a Trustee of the University of Tennessee.

All of us were in attendance at a party so red hot, it set fire to a downtown Knoxville hotel, got two previously angelic Little Sisters arrested for stealing a fire ax and a fireman's hat, and burned through our bail fund for the whole year. As to the cause of the fire, it's all a bit smoky, and I plead the better part of a fifth.

The fraternity had set fire to the same hotel three years before. We were nothing if not consistent.
Bob and I are both laughing now.
Just stories. On a beach in North Carolina. On a porch in Georgia. On a river in Tennessee. Engineers, an artist, an adman, a lawyer, a business owner, and entrepreneur. Husbands, fathers, grandfathers. Survivors now, we're lucky to be alive, and very lucky to have stories and laughter – and friendships – like that to share.
We didn't lose Bob Alley. We found him and each other a half-century ago at the University of Tennessee. Thank God.

– Dan Conaway

*"We were too young for that.
Are we ever old enough for that?"*

GODSPEED, HELEN. WE WERE THERE.

Her name was Helen Larkin.

She was a couple of years younger than me when she started at the University of Tennessee and pledged the same sorority my wife did a few years earlier. Two of her three older brothers were in my fraternity, Tucker, and Steve, And one of her two sisters, Libba, was in my high school class in Memphis.

Spring quarter of her freshman year, Helen would become a Little Sister of our fraternity. She sparkled.

Fall quarter of her sophomore year, her life, and the lives of everyone who knew and loved her would be reshaped in bent metal and broken glass in a tragic moment on a dark street in Knoxville. The lives of everyone in that car would forever change. One life ended there, two others would have to be rebuilt from broken parts, and Helen would disappear into a coma.

Ever since, I have never gone down the steep hill off Church Street to Neyland Drive just before the bridge that my heart didn't sink, that a sense of senseless loss didn't visit, that those in that car didn't come to mind.

We were too young for that. Are we ever old enough for that?

Helen's momma, Gloria Larkin, widowed young and mother of six, brought her home to Memphis and enrolled in nursing school so that she could help Helen gradually return to the light, neither of them ever giving up. All of Helen's family in Memphis and Atlanta made sure the light shined as bright as possible for Helen, never dimming her spirit despite considerable physical and neurological challenges.

NEVER OVER THE HILL

Gloria Larkin was one of the bravest, toughest, and most loving models for parenthood my life has known. A force. An inspiration.

Helen's arduous journey ended in 2018 and we were there at her funeral to wish her Godspeed in the next one, her challenges happily over.

Her brother, my close friend and fraternity brother, Steve, was there – who used to stand with me on the frat house porch waiting for two girls who were driving from Memphis together to see us, the two girls we're married to today.

Another fraternity brother, Pat Mahoney, was there – who was in that wreck almost 50 years ago – and who visited Helen regularly over these decades, in her last years every week, sometimes several times a week, always with flowers, or sneaking in a forbidden milkshake, or both. And often sneaking a walk outside without permission, wheeling Helen through a side door, both chuckling as they broke the rules, like the kids they were when that night wrecked her life and forever changed his.

Pat Mahoney is a loving lesson in loyalty, friendship, and purpose, and a reminder of the difference those things can make.

Many fraternity brothers were there, for Helen and the Larkins, and for each other – in recognition of that bright, cute girl we knew and of the formative, sometimes stupid, sometimes tragic, always fascinating, and unforgettable time we shared coming of age.

Greek letters and names don't matter, whether or not it's a fraternity or a sorority or a garden club doesn't matter, or a political party for that matter. What matters is being part of something that can support and comfort, correct and forgive, and love and laugh and cry with you, sometimes at the same time, while all the time helping navigate a larger, stormier sea.

This day, we were happy for Helen and to have known her and each other. It occurred to me that I wouldn't have known her or any of them or much of my life without our common bond.

Those who would legislate the end of fraternities and sororities should understand that the recklessness of youth wouldn't end with that legislation, only the peer support to survive it and the recognition of that support for a lifetime.

At UT, I met a courageous girl named Helen and some pretty terrific guys.

– Dan Conaway

"*Gini and the family watched, waited, and talked to him all the time with no response.*"

HEY, HOPE, HOW ARE YOU?

Healthcare isn't politics. It's not close votes or cold numbers or hot heads or independent scoring. Healthcare is someone in a bed, dependent on tubes and screens and strangers and mysteries and miracles.

Healthcare is reason for hope. Healthcare is survival. Or not.

I was attempting to visit a friend in extended care at Regional One in Memphis, somewhere in the hospital complex called Turner Tower. "Called what?" the parking lot attendant replied, and then added, "Got to be one of those."

"The those" were all the backs of all the buildings we were staring at, an architectural metaphor both for the disparate mess our healthcare system has become and for the navigation of same.

I followed someone in scrubs through a door and asked someone else in scrubs where Turner Tower was. She was kind enough to take me on a "short cut" through all sorts of swinging doors and down long hallways between buildings and by lots of people in nametags to an unmarked service elevator.

When the elevator doors opened, I walked around a corner and into Tem Mitchell's room.

I met Tem when we were both at UT. We were both majoring in architecture. That wouldn't last, but our friendship did.

We met when we shared a nude drawing class in the old Estabrook Hall. My talent was questionable, but the view was excellent. Tem was serious. I was, let's say, distracted. Tem would graduate with a design degree. I would graduate with the last of five majors.

NEVER OVER THE HILL

We both ended up in Memphis, and I later hired Tem as an art director and production manager in a couple of my ad agencies, and he's been a steady friend and reliable smile across my unsteady career.

When a bookkeeper's malfeasance cost me the last of those agencies, Tem cried when I made the announcement – not for the loss of his job but for pain he saw in my eyes and in the slump of my shoulders.

On a Saturday in 2017, he was playing with his grandkids on a Horseshoe Lake dock, about an hour from Memphis in Arkansas.

A couple of days later he was in the emergency room, and then ICU, conscious but barely, confused and in pain, and then in some sort of tortured, suspended state. His facial expressions were a map of a mind receiving awful signals and unable to verbally express them, his responses and movements were primal, and then they were almost nothing.

They didn't know what it was – some sort of encephalitis – and then came the diagnosis – West Nile Virus – for which there is no cure. Can mosquitoes ever leave us the hell alone? Gini and the family watched, waited, and talked to him all the time with no response. Reality became a visitor as well. Living wills became a subject. Recovery became a hope, and then a distant hope.

He was moved to extended care.

When you've known someone, laughed, and cried with someone, shared work and reward and loss with someone, since you were both impossibly young, that first meeting in Estabrook is suddenly as clear as yesterday·

"Are we supposed to draw or stare?" I whispered then. "Both," he answered.

You can't go, Tem. Class isn't over.

Then I heard he was better. Said something. Told Gini he loved her, knew names of family members, the name of his cat.

"Hey, Dan," Tem said when I walked into the room.

I cried. Not in the room, I was laughing in the room, but out in the hall as I retraced my steps. Scrubs #2 walked by again. "Are you okay?"

"Oh, yeah," I said, "I'm fine," a smile on my wet face.

Tem's long and tortuous journey is what healthcare is really about, not the indifference to millions upon millions who would never have an opportunity for recovery, who would die from a mosquito bite for want of insurance.

No family should have to go through what Tem's family has, but every family should have every chance to hear someone they love say "hey" again.

Hey, Tem.

– Dan Conaway

"He was Brownsville's favorite son, and Brownsville was his favorite place on earth."

LIFE IS A SONG

On the 50-mile drive over to Brownsville from Memphis, Marsha Thompson told us a story.

Homesick at UT, she really wanted a quick visit home to Lookout Mountain, so she asked fellow student and friend Ronnie Richards to take her.

She showed him around including a visit to her church. Ronnie made a beeline for the organ, opened it up – telling her that organists always keep the key in the same place – and fired it up, pulling out the stops and joyfully filling the big empty church with big, beautiful sound in an impromptu concert for two.

There was a lot of joy and big, beautiful sound to Ronnie's life.

The trip to Brownsville was for his funeral. Everyone in the car knew Ronnie in college a half century before this day. He was my big brother in the fraternity. He convinced me I could sing. I can't, but I did because of Ronnie. He convinced me I could co-direct a production with him. I didn't think I could, but I did because of Ronnie.

It's fair to say, no one in the car enjoyed every day then and since, even the bad ones, like he did. As his children – all four spoke at the service – all pointed out, he celebrated.

How was your day? "Terrific."
How was lunch? "Spectacular."
And toward the end, in pain, how was your morning? "Remarkable."

Lately, it may seem like I'm writing a lot about loss – God knows my dark suit is getting a workout – but I believe I'm actually writing about life. Nothing focuses your attention on the length and breadth of a shared journey and its shared meaning like the end of that journey.

Like its beginning, this one ended as a celebration of a person and place. Brownsville, Tennessee, and Ronnie Richards were inseparable – he, the town's biggest advocate – the town and everyone in it, his biggest friend.

He was Brownsville's favorite son, and Brownsville was his favorite place on earth.

He was in insurance, and real estate, and laughter and love.

He became the organist for the Baptist church in the eighth grade. Over his life, and sometimes over the same weekend, he was the organist for the Episcopal Church, the Presbyterian Church, the Synagogue, and the funeral home, and the life of a party.

We had a grand piano in the frat house. Ronnie made that happen. Come on, frat houses don't have grand pianos; they have chipped tables covered with cigarette burns and dried beer. We had those too, but that piano remained pristine.

Ronnie made that happen too, and we gathered around that piano and sang. Come on, frat houses gather around kegs. We had those, too, but nowhere near Ronnie's grand. What do you suppose made me think I could sing?

Ronnie. And the keg helped.

As I sat in the church before things commenced – actually in the standing room only fellowship hall because we got there just an hour and a half early and the church was already standing room only – the woman next to me, Peggy, talked about life in Brownsville.

"When we lived in Memphis, my husband would blow dry his hair on the way to church at stoplights. Here, it stays soaking wet. Two minutes." She continued, "Between our house and the square, maybe half a mile, I pass my dentist, my hairdresser, the ATM, the mail drop, the grocery store," this is my favorite part, "and the best gas station chicken in town."

Visits to small towns in the company of those who live there are common among those who go to state universities, and the closeness of life there can seem so compelling when they celebrate one of their own. This was a town-wide event, and the procession to the gravesite in outlying Nutbush stretched seemingly unbroken from the church to the cemetery.

In a wider world, the girl from Lookout Mountain next to me in the car was Marsha Goree Thompson, the mother-in-law of Peyton Manning, and the community of Nutbush is where Tina Turner was born.

In my world and that of my oldest friends, Marsha is the Sweetheart of my college fraternity and Nutbush is where our friend Ronnie Richards is buried.

Ford is building their largest automotive plant in the world just outside Brownsville, and Brownville is about to be where all-electric Ford 150 Lightning trucks will be from.

To us, Brownsville is where Ronnie Richards was from.

Life in a world of friends is worth living.

– Dan Conaway

Spring 1975 graduation, Chancellor Reese and Bill Haltom

AND SO, IT ENDS

A diploma is in one sense an official notice that
you have completed the necessary requirements
for whatever degree is thereby referenced,
so goodbye and good luck.

It is in another sense a recipe.
The ingredients are there,
now go make something with them.

AND SO, IT BEGINS

Like any recipe, the first few attempts will not
represent everything made or possible, thank God,
and both process and result will improve
with time, judgment, and experience.

For most of you reading this book,
the key ingredients are grown on a hill
and only grow better with age:

Orange and White.

"*I wasn't going to ask my father, who was proudly in attendance at my ceremonies, to pay my parking tickets as a graduation present.*"

A DIPLOMA, JUST THE TICKET

I will never forget the moment when I received my diploma from the University of Tennessee. Well, I thought it was my diploma.

It was at the commencement exercises at Stokely Athletic Center in the spring of 1975. I proudly walked up on to the stage, shook hands with President Boling and Chancellor Reese, and was handed a cylinder that I assumed contained my degree.

When I got back to my seat on the floor of the arena, I couldn't wait to open that cylinder and pull out that piece of paper I had passed 180 quarter hours to receive. But when I opened the cylinder, there was no diploma inside. Instead, so help me, there was a note that read as follows:

Your diploma has been temporarily withheld due to unpaid student parking tickets. Please report to Room 201 of the Administration building to pay your parking tickets and receive your diploma.

The bad news Is that I had over $200 in unpaid parking tickets, and even worse, I didn't have the money to pay for them. I wasn't going to ask my father, who was proudly in attendance at my ceremonies, to pay my parking tickets as a graduation present.

I was tempted to forego my diploma and just frame the note saying my diploma was "temporarily withheld." The note didn't say I didn't graduate or have a degree. In fact, it said I had a degree, and my diploma was simply being held for me in some administration office.

Some UT students graduate Summa Cum Laude. Some graduate Magna Cum Laude. I graduated Laude Have Mercy with the highest number of parking tickets.

NEVER OVER THE HILL

I did manage to get my diploma. I refuse to answer the question of whether I paid all my parking tickets, on the grounds that it may incriminate me.

I'll take the fifth, a familiar phrase to many college students.

Three years later I had a second commencement day when I graduated from law school.

At this commencement, my diploma was not temporarily withheld. As a law student I had learned how to avoid student parking tickets. That's my story, and I'm sticking to it.

Commencement day is a joyful one for college graduates. It is a day of celebration with your fellow students, and photo ops with your parents, siblings, or other loved ones. And, by definition, it is the day one's life in the real world commences.

I was ready and anxious on commencement day for the next era of my life to, in fact, commence.

But by the fall after my graduation, I felt a yearning to head back to The Hill. I missed my wonderful Alma Mater.

And so that fall, I went home to The Hill on a weekend called "Homecoming." And I have been making that wonderful trip back home at least once a year for more than 40 years.

– Bill Haltom

> *"I showed Dad the budget I'd worked up. I can still hear how loud he laughed as he poured two jiggers of Jim Beam, and we knocked them back in the kitchen."*

I DO, SHE DID, AND WE STILL ARE

"Dad," I said, "Nora and I are getting married."

"Congratulations," son, "she's a sweetheart," he paused, "How do you plan to eat?"

Dad was such a romantic. But it was a fair question. How indeed?

That conversation was held the spring of my junior year. We were engaged during spring break. I don't remember asking, Nora doesn't remember saying yes. It seems to have occurred over hamburgers in a loud new Memphis hot spot called Friday's in Memphis, the second one in the world, following the first in New York.

Probably something like this ...

"Wave at the waiter, I need another beer," I yelled, "getting married might be a good idea."

"I need more pickles," she yelled back, "maybe so."

We were such romantics. But we're coming up on 53 years as of this writing. We've lasted longer than that Friday's.

I told Dad that I'd saved about 300 bucks, and Nora's state job would transfer to Knoxville. She had graduated from Memphis State in January as an English major. Evidently, that was just what the welfare department was looking for and she was hired.
She had already been promoted to case supervisor and that came with a raise to $480 a month. I had the hundred bucks a month Dad sent me, and a little of this-and-that money I had started making freelancing copy for radio stations.

I showed Dad the budget I'd worked up. I can still hear how loud he laughed as he poured two jiggers of Jim Beam, and we knocked them back in the kitchen.

"Will you be my best man?"

He gave me a hug, and we knocked two more back. He did not give me a raise.

We decided on a December date since I would be on Christmas break. The date was set for December 19, 1970.

Her bridesmaids would be then Edith Wilkinson and then Mamel Cole, and her maid of honor would be then Linda Nowlin. They were three of the four friends who gave Nora a Siamese cat named after them ... Klem ... Karen, Linda, Edith and Mamel. Klem would try and kill me several times while Nora and I were dating.

Klem was such a romantic.

My groomsmen would be freshman roommate and lifelong friend Pete Bale, high school friend and fraternity brother Jeff Michael, and fraternity brother, roommate, and best friend Bob Alley.
Ushers would be Nora's cousins, Brad Tomlinson, a senior at W&L, and George Tomlinson, a sophomore and All-SEC defensive back for Vanderbilt.
I look at those wedding pictures today, and we all look like we were still in high school faking a wedding for a school play.

We were married in the chapel at Second Presbyterian Church in Memphis, a relatively small wedding but a big reception at Chickasaw Country Club.
Around Thanksgiving, I stuck an invitation to the reception on the bulletin board of the fraternity house. Since the wedding was during Christmas break, a bundle of brothers showed up from all over west

Tennessee. Early, in fact. By the time the wedding party got to the reception, the club had run out of champagne and had to scramble for more.

Some had decided since they were in town, they'd come to the wedding, too, not letting lack of a formal invitation stand in the way.

Meanwhile, Dad, the minister and I, were waiting in a small room at the front of the chapel. Dr. Russell, beloved head minister at the church, had become very ill, so his assistant, Dr. Hazelwood, would be marrying us. He was a gray-haired, humorless fellow in thick black glasses under a frown.

Dad broke the nervous silence in the little room by reaching inside his morning coat and producing a silver flask, "Let's toast the proceedings," he said cheerfully.

"Well," said an irritated Hazelwood, rising from his chair and literally shaking his robe with a huff, "if that is alcohol, I cannot remain."

"See you in there," Dad said, raising the flask and winking at me.

When Dad and I came out and took our position in front of the packed chapel, I realized if I met the eyes of the assembly, including the frat brothers wanting desperately for me to do just that, I might just lose it, so I fixed my eyes – trance-like I'm told – on a spot above the chapel doors.

When Nora came through those doors, I lowered my eyes and looked only at her, knowing we'd get through this together.

And so we have.

Nora and I were going to honeymoon for three whole nights in New Orleans, driving ourselves there after the reception, spending the night in Jackson, Mississippi, on the way.
Heralding the fashion nap the country would take for the decade of the 70s, allow me to describe my going away outfit:

A navy blue and white houndstooth check suit, with checks big enough to play checkers on and lapels damn near lapping my shoulders, fake belt in the back, western flap pockets in the front with woven leather buttons. A French-blue, French-cuffed shirt with fake emerald cufflinks. A red-white-and-blue, chain-patterned tie so wide it could double as a tablecloth. A pair of patent leather, blue and yellow – yes, yellow – cap toe shoes. Please.

Nora, however, was lovely in a heavily embroidered pearl gray and navy wool coat her mother had bought for her at Bergdorf Goodman – a coat way out of our budget – then and now. It was a coat that covered her dress below, and was still several inches above her knee.

On the drive to Jackson, there was no interstate for the 50-plus miles from Vaiden to Canton. Just as we entered that stretch, a heavy fog descended and reduced our progress to a crawl. Nora was drinking a Tab from a Styrofoam cup – her drink of choice – and rolled down the window to throw about half of it out into the gray blanket, only to have the whole of that half blow right back in and all over that Bergdorf Goodman coat. That made the night even darker.

The romantic honeymoon began.

We arrived in New Orleans the next morning. I had made reservations at the Maison de Ville, a lovely boutique hotel in the French Quarter that shared a high courtyard wall with the Court of Two Sisters. I remembered it from a stay with my parents years before, and while he didn't give me a raise on my monthly college stipend, my father did make a present of our Mason de Ville stay.

I had called the hotel two weeks before, and asked for a dozen long-stem roses to be in our room on our arrival.

And so they were, in a beautiful vase. Black, limp, and dead as a hammer. Evidently, they had put them in that room the day I called, and it hadn't been booked since.

The romantic honeymoon continued.

NEVER OVER THE HILL

The room had a 14-foot ceiling, brocade wall coverings, antique furnishings, and a view of courtyard below and the vine-covered wall of the Court of Two Sisters beyond. It had no TV, no shower, no room service, and absolutely no sound. Funeral homes are livelier.

We checked out the next morning and moved into the Downtowner on Bourbon Street a block away.

We enjoyed the finer aspects of the Crescent City:

Dining from the windows of Takee-Outee and from the Lucky Dogs, the rolling painted sheet-metal hot dogs. Splitting a shrimp po boy at Felix's, and half a muffuletta from Central Grocery. Drinks and modern dance at a jiggle joint, live theater for *Nobody Likes a Smart Ass* at the Absinthe House, and live music for whatever you drop in the hat everywhere.

The likes of Galatoire's would have to wait for other visits and gainful employment.

Our last night, we wandered into the Desire Oyster Bar. We had a dozen on the half shell, a basket of crabs we cracked open with the butt of my beer bottle, and a pound of boiled shrimp.

When we were done and I asked for the check, the waiter said it was all on the house. Seems they had noticed we were newlyweds by our attention to each other, and dinner was a wedding present.

Now that, friends, was plenty romantic enough for us.

Who are we to question the employees of the Desire Oyster Bar?

Love can be seen, and love can last.

– **Dan Conaway**

"Friends of ours living there were fooling around in the hall of their apartment, never mind what they were doing, and fell through the wall into the apartment next door. There were no studs. Not a few studs, or badly spaced studs. No studs. Just sheetrock stapled to thin wooden strips. The plumbing had the same reliability."

NEVER OVER THE HILL

STRING PULLING, LIVING WITH JOCKS, AND CHAUCER

My uncle by marriage was Frank Ahlgren.

That probably doesn't mean anything to you – or to me either growing up – since his wife, my aunt, and the sister of my mother, were in a lifelong battle, and Uncle Frank didn't seem to have much use for me, or anybody else for that matter except Uncle Frank.

He was, however, a big deal in certain circles, say, the University of Tennessee. He was a Trustee, and had been one since the college was laid out in 1794, or so it seemed.

He was the editor, master, and commander of *The Commercial Appeal* in Memphis since its founding in the mid-19th century, or so it seemed.

He was one of those men who looked like he was born at about age 50, and looked more than a little like a bulldog. In fact, he owned a long succession of bulldogs, second only to Georgia.

Or so all of that seemed to a little boy.

Once when I was that little boy and playing on his living room floor, he and one of those bulldogs were across the room, he reading a paper and the bulldog by his chair. I looked back and forth between the two of them several times noting the similarity, and then noting that Uncle Frank had lowered his paper and caught me in the act.

That was one of the few times I saw him smile, perhaps the only time.

Guy Northrop, longtime writer and editorial page editor for *The Commercial Appeal*, once told me at a cocktail party, "You know, Dan,

I've worked for your uncle for more than 30 years and come to know him affectionately as Mr. Ahlgren."

You see, Frank Ahlgren came from his native Wisconsin in the 1920s to his new job at *The Commercial Appeal*, stepping off the train in Memphis in jungle-hot August in a heavy, three-piece white wool suit.

He was a bad mood ever after.

Fast forward to the spring of 1970 and my approaching marriage. I had applied for married student housing for the winter and spring quarters of 1971, anticipating graduation in June of 1971.

Way ahead of the application deadline.

You see, married student housing at UT was a crapshoot, and we wanted to be one of the first in line for the following academic year.

You could get one of the brand-new – ugly, but brand-new – married student apartment towers near campus. You could get one of the married student garden apartment complexes here and there, all from very nice to okay.

Or you could get Golf Range.

The commercial developer who built Golf Range Apartments on a – failed golf range – would have to have spent a lot more money building them just to be called cheap. They weren't close to code, or anything you'd want to be close to, you know, on cheap land where somebody would build – a golf range. Even the weeds that substituted for grass looked tired and neglected. The apartments failed, too, and UT snapped them up.

Friends of ours living there were fooling around in the hall of their apartment, never mind what they were doing, and fell through the wall into the apartment next door.

275

NEVER OVER THE HILL

There were no studs. Not a few studs, or badly spaced studs. No studs. Just sheetrock stapled to thin wooden strips. The plumbing had the same reliability.

As instructed, we checked off our choices in order of preference – one through four. For giggles, our first choice was Woodlawn, the fanciest, where married athletes, and married student children of state legislators and megadonors lived, and then we had three realistic choices after that.

Golf Range wasn't on our list. Golf Range was what we got. And they didn't let us know until the beginning of fall quarter before our wedding in December.

I hadn't seen or spoken to Uncle Frank in the three years I'd been at UT. I don't think he even knew I was at UT, and if he did, I wasn't the one who told him.

Some years before when my oldest brother Frank – named after Dad, most assuredly not after Uncle Frank – was at UT for his first two years in college, he visited Uncle Frank when he was in Knoxville for a UT Board of Trustees meeting.

More accurately, brother Frank visited Uncle Frank's hotel suite when he wasn't there, brought along a few of his Kappa Sig fraternity brothers, cleaned out the well-stocked liquor cabinet, and helped themselves to the covered dishes on the table. Uncle Frank was about to host a cocktail party for a few of the trustees.

Imagine his surprise.

Frank left a note, a note both famous and infamous depending on who in the family you talk to:

"Thanks, Uncle Frank. We were a bit dry."

No need to sign it.

I wasn't anxious to continue the family tradition as I imagine Uncle Frank wasn't either, but I needed help.

I called my uncle. I explained my situation to what seemed to be a silent phone. No congratulations on the coming wedding. No how's the family. No warm and fuzzy how's college going questions. Maybe the line was dead.

"Not sure I can help," he said, and the call was over.

I told Nora not to be hopeful, and we began training for living somewhere without ever leaning against the walls.

A couple of weeks later, I got a letter from the university.

"Our apologies," it began. "There was a mistake made when your application for married student housing was received. You have been assigned to Woodlawn," and so on, continuing with the details.

Sweet, lovable Uncle Frank had come through.

This is how I learned about string pulling, an exercise in influence and privilege. I would see it, and continue to see it, the rest of my life. Who you know, and who you're related to, very often proving to be more important than who you actually are.

Yet, I gleefully accepted the largesse. Funny how things like that seem to be okay if you're the one pulling the strings.

And so it was that our married life began at Woodlawn, in a one bedroom, furnished, $95 a month, garden apartment on Woodlawn Pike just off Chapman Highway up on a kudzu-covered bluff overlooking Shoney's. Swimming pool, tennis court, and Jim Weatherford as a neighbor, among other notables.

NEVER OVER THE HILL

He was on the cover of Sports Illustrated in 1967 breaking up a pass to an Alabama receiver under the headline, "TENNESSEE OVERWHELMS ALABAMA." Yes, we did. In Legion Field. Five interceptions, and I was there and saw every one of them.

That cover, blown up, dominated a wall in his apartment right below us. I think I bowed the first time I met him. I also think he let me.

We arrived on New Year's Eve in a rented truck shared with another couple from Memphis, fraternity brother Steve Brandon – Stick – and new wife Chris, who were married the same day as we were. I never asked Stick what strings he pulled.

We had used some of our meager savings to buy two necessities – our first two pieces of furniture – a damn good mattress and a color TV on sale.

The Brandons joined us as we ate Krystals and watched Tennessee beat Air Force in the Sugar Bowl on our new TV. It was a console with a whopping 18" screen. We had it for another 20 years.

We went to K-Mart for the other start-up necessities - a spatula, paper towels, toilet paper, salt and pepper, eggs, bacon, bread, cereal, peanuts, chips, peanut butter, Cheetos, Krispy Kreme, Tab, milk, beer on special, and, of course, a parakeet.

His name was Chaucer.

He was a failure as a bird. He couldn't fly, but he knew he was supposed to, and he had heart. Watching him try, taking off from his cage door, crashing to the floor, launching again to land on the picture frame above the couch, and then repeating the whole process in reverse was – God help me – more entertaining than the Star Trek re-runs on TV.

Winter and spring quarters came and went pretty quietly.

Nora took the car to work, I took the UT bus to campus. Stick and I laid out a wiffle-ball golf course winding through the pines on the hill below our apartments, and we – and the other All-American jocks – would play a few holes before dinner.

Nights out included the all-you-can-eat fish special at Shoney's, and going to the frat house to play bridge, or the pinball machine in the basement. I knew which back leg to prop up so we could play all night for free.

Fraternity brother Mason Blake worked at the liquor store just down the hill from our apartment on Chapman Highway. We had an unofficial buy-one-get-one arrangement. Keep that to yourself. Mason has been very successful, and while I'm sure nobody has warrants, let's not take any chances.

Come to think of it, that might have been string pulling, too.

We had a blast. We didn't have two nickels at the same time, but we saved more money as a percentage of our income over those six months than we have over any six-month period since.

However, neither one of us has ever had another bite of fish at Shoney's.

I graduated, but I didn't walk. I'd been offered a job, and when asked if I could start on a certain day, I said, "of course." That day was graduation day, but I wasn't going to take a chance. If he wanted me to start then, I would start then.

And so I did, and had my diploma sent to me.

When it arrived, I showed it to Dad. When I graduated from high school, he shook my hand, gave me a hug, congratulated me, and told me that I had four years from that night to show him another diploma.

When we came home, and started work, and I didn't have one, he might have been a bit skeptical. Sure enough, it showed up, encased in wood, shellacked and shiny.

Five majors and a minor in psychology I didn't even know I had, four years, three summers in night school, more than 200 hours, at least that many adventures, a break-up, a wedding, and friends and memories for a lifetime.

There you go, Dad, and thanks. You drove a nervous kid over there, and a young married man drove back.

There's a lot packed in that diploma; above every desk I've had since it arrived.

– Dan Conaway

"We beat Florida like a rented mule ... perhaps more like a drowned gator ... Dwight Teeter had fallen in love with our brand of UT football, Hallie's place in the next year's freshman class had been baptized in the rain on the shore of the Tennessee River, and Phil Fulmer rose from the water as the new head coach of the Volunteers."

DWIGHT WAS RIGHT, AND THE HALL OF FAME

Dr. Dwight Teeter came from the other UT, you know, the other one with orange and white for colors, the one in Texas.

He was the brand-new Dean of the College of Communications in 1992 when we met, and was overseeing his first meeting of the board of visitors of the college that fall. I was on that board for 30 years, appointed by professor and friend, the late Don Hileman, when he became Dean.

We had a weekend meeting every fall, and, of course, a football game. That weekend, I brought my daughter, Hallie, along. She was a high school senior, a very good student, and she was considering colleges. James Madison was in the running, maybe Chapel Hill in there somewhere, and Tennessee was leading.

I had work to do. As far as I was concerned, this was a recruiting trip and an official visit.

Dwight invited us to join him in College of Communications seats – upper deck, west side in the curve of the end zone, very first row. We were hanging out over the field. Nora wasn't along for this one. It was us and the dean.

It was the first game Dwight was to attend. It was the Florida game, people. Florida. Steve Spurrier's Florida, and Phil Fulmer's Tennessee. He was the interim coach, in for Johnny Majors who was out with heart issues.

It was the Florida game in 1992.

Dwight got into it. Sitting next to us, he had no choice. I had convinced him to leave his sport coat in the meeting room, and dug an extra hat out of my car. It started out hot, and then it rained. We had the lead. And it poured. We built the lead, and we almost couldn't see the other end of the field.

Somewhere close by, Noah was building an arc.

Our feet were literally under water. If there was a drain for that bottom row, it was clogged. We purposefully stomped our feet to make waves, jumping up and down, screaming in the downpour.

Dwight's dress shirt was soaked to transparency, his dress shoes were ruined, the handkerchief he used to wipe his glasses was now a sopping wet rag.

And he didn't care.

We beat Florida like a rented mule ... perhaps more like a drowned gator ... Dwight Teeter had fallen in love with our brand of UT football, Hallie's place in the next year's freshman class had been baptized in the rain on the shore of the Tennessee River, and Phil Fulmer rose from the water as the new head coach of the Volunteers.

An eventful day.

Dwight and I became good friends over the years. Among his many accomplishments and interests, he became involved with the Tennessee Newspaper Hall of Fame, housed at the University of Tennessee since 1969, and in the College of Communications since the college's inception.

The Hall of Fame inductees are, in fact, pictured along the hall of the third floor of the college – considered actually the main floor since its curved glass walls front on Circle Park. Walking along that hall to a classroom to deliver a guest lecture in 1979, I happened to glance up and see someone familiar.

NEVER OVER THE HILL

My late uncle, Cal Alley, staring back at me, Hall of Fame inductee Number 21, inducted in 1979. He was the editorial cartoonist for *The Commercial Appeal* in Memphis, widely recognized and at the height of his career when he died of cancer in 1970. My mother's brother, he worked for editor Frank Ahlgren – the iron-willed dictator of the paper and the Uncle Frank I described in the story before this one.

In other words, Uncle Calvin had to get in a fight with his brother-in-law boss every day in order to get his cartoon in the paper. That alone should have given him consideration for the Hall.

Anyway, there he was. I didn't know it. Neither of my two older brothers knew it. My mother and father didn't know it. I assume Uncle Calvin's wife knew it, but at least three of his five kids I spoke with didn't.

Our family, as you may have gathered, was not close.

Earlier in 1992 than the fall football game, Dwight, the new Dean had gotten in touch with me about the Hall of Fame. He was pursuing and recommending someone else for induction and was contacting me for help.

His choice was J.P. Alley, my grandfather. My mother's father. Uncle Calvin's father. Uncle Frank's father-in-law. Like his son after him, also the editorial cartoonist for *The Commercial Appeal*. And far more famous as an editorial cartoonist in his day than Uncle Calvin, with a daily cartoon syndicated in hundreds of papers, often on their front pages, and with a Pulitzer Prize shared with the paper's editorial department for their fight against the Ku Klux Klan in 1923.

Dwight knew all about that, both as a student and as a teacher of journalism history.

Why, Dwight wondered, Why would J.P.'s son be inducted before him? Why had he not been considered?

Because of the cartoon he fathered, I offered as explanation. It was a one-panel ink drawing of an everyman, working man philosopher, offering his daily observations of human foibles and human nature as it passed by.

It was called Hambone, and Hambone was a Black man, speaking in dialect.

Inappropriate as it became, Hambone was beloved in its time, and its creator was a champion against the KKK at great personal risk to his family. My grandfather died in 1934, yet Hambone continued beyond his death, written by my grandmother, and drawn by Uncle Calvin until its cancellation in 1968.

That continuation should be questioned far more than his creation.

Dwight helped me come to grips with that, and I joined in the effort to get Granddad in the Hall.
When the effort was successful, I softened in my opinion of Uncle Frank and convinced him to make the trip to Knoxville and give the induction speech for his father-in-law.

Dwight helped me to come around on that, too.

Dwight was right.

Thus, Frank Ahlgren was there in 1993 for the induction of Number 30 in the Hall of Fame, James Pinckney Alley. Uncle Frank died two years after making that speech at the age of 83.

And we weren't through, Dwight and I, and my family.

He stepped down from Dean in 2006 and returned to research and teaching. I got in touch and asked if he would help me pursue another possible inductee for the Hall.

NEVER OVER THE HILL

One who had assumed the role of Editor at the age of 33 at a major daily in Tennessee and held the job until his retirement 32 years later. One who covered the Japanese surrender on the deck of the USS Missouri. One who fought Jim Crow, and was a major force in the Accrediting Council certifying journalism and mass communication education programs. One who was a University of Tennessee Trustee for 27 years, and instrumental ... in fact, key ... to starting the College of Communications.

One who wrote this:

"An editor is under a special obligation to do more than anyone else because a newspaper office has an amazing opportunity to translate ideas into practice. In a sense the newspaper is not the editor's but the property of the community."

Frank Richard Ahlgren – friendly, effervescent Uncle Frank.

So it was, that he became Number 45 in the Hall of Fame, inducted in 2007. And so it was, coming full circle, I was able to pull a string, and start a process, and pay back a debt.

Over the years, Dwight and I would talk often. I was honored to have him as a friend, and especially honored that he would ask for my advice about this and that, fundraising for the college, positioning and marketing for the college.

And jokes.

Dwight Teeter died in 2015. Over his career, he taught six Pulitzer Prize winners. In his obituary, this was noted: "He sent Associated Press photographer Neal Ulevich a congratulatory note after his Pulitzer Prize award, jokingly taking credit for Ulevich's success. Ulevich, ever the quick wit, responded that he had to settle for a Pulitzer, saying that knowing Teeter cost him the Nobel Prize."

Dwight co-authored a definitive textbook, "Law of Mass Communications, Freedom and Control of Print and Broadcast Media," 13 editions. "A real page-turner," Dwight called it. In my copy of the eighth edition, there's a handwritten note:

"For Dan Conaway – a favorite teacher – from Dwight Teeter"

That book sits on my desk, and always will.

Down the hall and around the corner from the Hall of Fame photos is the college auditorium, beautifully redone as part of one of those fundraising efforts. Dedication of individual seats was a part of that. On the arm of one are three plaques reading as follows:

Daniel Edwin Conaway, BS, Communications, 1971
Hallie Elizabeth Conaway, BS. Communications, 1997
Gaines Alley Conaway, BS, Communications, 2003

That's my Hall of Fame.

– *Dan Conaway*

ROOSTER
SCRATCH
PRESS

Made in the USA
Columbia, SC
15 November 2023